A FUNNY THING HAPPENED ON MY WAY TO THE CRYPT!

MARILYN ZAPATA

ATAPAZ PRESS

A FUNNY THING HAPPENED ON MY WAY TO THE CRYPT!

First Edition: July 2016

The information in this book is true and complete to the best of our knowledge. All recommendations are made without guarantee on the part of the author. The author and publisher disclaim any liability in connection with the use of this information.

This book is dedicated in loving memory to Gloria Hander Lyon, a fellow writer, a good friend, and my publishing mentor, and without whose knowledge, generosity and friendship I would still be saying, "You know, one of these days I'd really like to write a book."

(1)

Before deciding to write another book, I debated the genre of this venture. Should it be a coffee table book, a how-to book (you can't be serious), another photo book, a sequel to the best seller, "Seven Wonders of a Senior's World" (okay, maybe not a best seller, but a good seller; okay, maybe not a good seller, but a seller, nonetheless) or should I attempt to write the Great American/Mexican Novel?

I went to a writer's web site to find the answer. They asked the question: "What is your target audience?" Never having thought of that before, I wasn't sure on this one. My first response was: "Everyone." The next day the genre question was answered for me by an unlikely source. A friend said to me, "I absolutely love your books" ... I blushed and humbly thanked her, and then she finished her sentence ... "the stories are perfect bathroom reading." And "Wham," I had found my niche, a whole genre previously left untapped and targeted only by Reader's Digest.

Then, being me, I went even further. I decided to rate each story with a (1), (2), (3) or (4). (1) and (2) being self-explanatory, (3) being for the chronic sitters, and (4) being for those who don't want to respond to their spouse pounding on the door. (Brighter heads prevailed, and my editor deleted all the numbers, so it'll be a "crap shoot" as to which story you will read.)

But wait, there's more. At the end of each story, I have added many asterisks (***************) indicating, "DON'T FORGET TO FLUSH!"

****

SENIOR LIVING AND LAUGHING!

In my first "fluff" book, **"The Seven Wonders of a Senior's World, (Who, What, Where, When, Why, Whether and Which?)"**, I planned on writing a collection of short stories told by my friends about "senior moments" a/k/a "brain farts" or "SMAs" (Senior Moment Adventures), but I felt obliged to introduce the book with some of my own flabbergasted experiences. And, as usual, I couldn't stop, so the book turned out to be "all about me," but I knew my material well and "they" do say to write what you know. Plus, I have been a life-long, card-carrying SMA person since my conception and would make the perfect poster woman for said affliction. "Nuf said."

The fact is: I learn something new every day but that means, since my mind is full to capacity, that I have to forget something. So, just in case in later years, I don't remember what a wonderful, fun-filled life I led and all the joyous people I met and befriended, I'll have printed proof of the good times and enjoy them all over again in the reading. So, here again, this second book is about me but then morphs into stories of my friends.

I want to add a disclaimer here: No seniors were harmed in the writing of this book. And any resemblance to a real person, living or dead, is purely non-coincidental.

****

In retrospect, this collection just might help ease the worries and embarrassment felt by many "age-challenged" individuals who are just beginning this journey into the "hereafter" ... as in "What am I here after?" Take heart, it's clear there's fun to be had in "senior moments."

****

HAVE YOU HEARD THIS ONE?

This year, Art, my husband, finally talked me into going to the Houston Home and Garden Show with him. I thought there would be nothing to interest me, but I was wrong. When we entered the big auditorium, there was a booth right in front with four or five white-robed "doctors" milling about. The sign read: "Free Hearing Test Today!"

Wow, I thought. This would be a great opportunity to have Art's hearing checked. For years, I had begged him to go have it tested, though I was talking to a deaf ear (or was it selected hearing?). He really couldn't hear me 50 percent of the time, and he still wouldn't admit this fact and had dug in his heels about having it tested.

Now was, indeed, the time. We were among the first patrons to enter into the show and nothing was happening; booths were only just being set up. There were no other customers at this hearing booth, and Art knew that I was doing him a favor by even coming to this show, so there was no way out. When I said, "Let's do it," he had to say, "Oh, okay," but he didn't have to say it like he meant it. And he didn't.

The test was meticulous and took about 20 minutes for each of us in our own capsule. It reminded me of the $64,000 Question, a TV show from the 1950s, where the contestant was locked in a soundproof booth and left there to sweat it out while his opponent answered the questions.

We both completed the test at the same time, and as we walked out of our respective booths, another doctor (or at least he wore a white coat) approached us and said, "Mrs. and Mr. Zapata, have a seat over here. And I'll tell you your results."

We sat down on cushy chairs, and he looked seriously at Art. Good, I thought, here it comes, the moment of hearing truth. "Mr. Zapata, I have to tell you that you have hearing quite adequate for your age and it will be a while before you will have to come visit us again!"

Damn, I thought, what a crock. I knew better. These were obvious charlatans, but why would they not want the business they could get from a positive test? I didn't have long to ruminate on this fact, because the doctor then turned to me.

"Mrs. Zapata, you, on the other hand, are going to need a hearing aid for your left ear." "WHAT?" I sputtered. He said again, in a louder tone, "Mrs. Zapata, you're going to need a hearing aid for your left ear." AND HE PATTED MY HAND. This time I muffled my "WHAT."

I was busy mentally damning those sensory gods, always playing tricks on me, but I waited for the guy to smile and admit there had been a mistake, but he never did. Then I turned to Art for my spousal support, and there spread across his face was the combination of an "I told you so" and "I knew it all along" smile with an overlap of the Cheshire cat grin.

I couldn't get out of that place quick enough. I didn't hear them on purpose, as they tried to talk to me and hand me the information to come in for a visit and get fitted for a "damn" trumpet!!!! But I'll never hear the end of it from Art.

****

ANOTHER DOG GONE EMERGENCY!

Art walked into the bedroom holding his head: "I don't feel so well. I've got that darn vertigo again."

My first thought was to rush him to the hospital, since this guy never complains about anything ... I take that back. He never complains about his body parts since I do enough of that for both of us. "Do you think we should go to the hospital?" I asked. This was a test. I knew if he said, "Yes," then he really was in dire straits.

"I don't know. Maybe. I don't want to clog up an emergency room, though, so maybe I'll wait it out a while."

I knew then that there really was something wrong and I needed to take action. "You know," I said, "I think I saw a new emergency clinic that opened up down by our old tennis club. That might be a good place to go. It'd only take a few minutes to get you there."

He was already putting on his jacket to leave. I felt really thankful and proud that I had spotted the sign a few days earlier and put it in my memory bank. Art felt the same way. He said, "I'm glad you knew about this place, since that's just perfect."

And off we went. I drove slowly since I didn't want his head to spin any more than necessary plus he usually was not a good passenger with me behind the wheel. But this time I knew he was concerned about his condition and still dizzy and distracted, since he had not one comment to make about my driving.

We pulled into the parking lot of the strip center clinic and found a spot right in front - kismet! I ran around to the passenger side of the car to help him out, wondering why he hadn't already opened his door.

He just sat there stoically. Oh, no, I thought, he can't even walk in. But then I looked at his face. He was giving me his "look." And when he saw that that wasn't enough, he said, "Look," and pointed up at the marquee.

The sign read in LARGE letters: "EMERGENCY VETERINARY CLINIC!"

I stammered, "Well, maybe you could ..." -- and he interrupted me: "Don't even think about it, let alone say it. Let's go to the hospital ... NOW!"

****

ART'S PSUEDO 50TH!

In September 1996, I started gathering my forces. This was going to be the mother of all surprises: I would throw Art a 50th birthday party, unbeknownst to him, in Monterrey, Mexico. For his 40th birthday, I had given him two surprise parties, with his real present being skydiving lessons – which he loved and which I watched with sweaty palms and a thumping heart as he jumped to his death (as it turned out, he didn't die, his chute opened) but had he bounced (skydiver's term), it would have been my fault. Now, this was going to be lots easier to watch but also harder to keep secret.

Since we share the same birthday day, October 17th, it's easy to remember when to celebrate. What's hard to remember are our ages. There's a six-year difference in our years -- the wrong way, I might add -- but I can quickly calculate our ages at any given decade by subtracting 1941 from the current year and then subtracting one if I haven't had my birthday yet for my age, and then subtracting six and adding one for Art's – my own invented formula that I had used successfully time and time again during the ages.

My plans were laid. I hired a bus and driver, plus a tour guide, out of San Antonio to deliver us to

Monterrey and show us around. It was only $135 per person for two nights, everything included. Next I just had to corral the people, which wouldn't be hard if Art wasn't around, but he always seemed to be at the house ... but then, again, I guess he lived there. This was before Al Gore created cyberspace and I had to do everything surreptitiously by my land line phone. Had Art learned of my plans, his hermit tendencies would have surfaced and he would have glued himself to the couch and told me to cancel all plans.

People were coming from all over: Two couples from Kansas, an octet of couples from Corpus Christi where we used to live, some of Art's family from Houston, and 20 or so miscellaneous friends from Friendswood. I made black burlap armbands for everyone to wear, dyed "cascarones" (confetti eggs) black and filled them with black confetti and made batches and batches of frozen margaritas, all under the unsuspecting and/or unregistering eyes of my husband.

The scheme was for us all to meet at 6:00 a.m. in San Antonio at the bus lot. But how could I make it all believable so that my non-gullible husband would fall for it? I told him that I wanted to go on a bus trip because my oldest friends were coming to visit from Kansas, and I wanted them to see Mexico; and, if we took the bus, we could drink and have a good time with them. It sounded plausible and it worked. Everyone who had any contact with Art had been warned to keep this high-level plot secret. He never found out. Never suspected. Everything appeared to be working out perfectly.

That is until three days before D-Day, departure day, when I came home sore from a tough tennis match. Art offered to give me a massage, so I lay down and while he kneaded, I almost dozed off but he hit a nerve and I jumped. He said, "Old Lady! You've never been this old before."

"Well," I said, "you're going to find out about being old. You're finally turning 50!!!"

There was a pause. And then he said the fateful words, "Yeah, but not until next year!"

Although almost asleep, my eyes shot open. I could hardly believe it! He was in denial, I thought. It happens to us all. I said, "No. You're going to be 50 in a few days!"

"No," he insisted, "I'm only going to be 49. Figure it out yourself. You're going to be 55. And I am six years younger, you know." (He loved saying that, but in reality, in dog years he had rushed past me a decade ago.)

I didn't speak. I couldn't. My head was spinning like Linda Blair's in the Exorcist, and my thoughts were running wild: It was too late to cancel the party, too late to call off the people, too late to stop the bus. I had ditty bags assembled to give everyone. There were 50 black balloons in my suitcase that said he was turning 50. And balloons don't lie. My final thought was: "I'm just going to go ahead with the party and just pretend he's going to be 50, and maybe no one will be the wiser."

I decided I wouldn't tell anyone I'd made this huge mistake. Fifty-five(my age) minus six (years difference) plus one (to make up the difference) equals 50. My system couldn't be wrong. But it was.

A friend from Corpus called to make more arrangements and quizzed me about details and I just had to 'fess up and admit my mistake to her. She said, "Don't worry about it. We're going to have fun anyway."

The big day arrived. At 6:00 a.m. precisely we entered the bus parking lot. The big hulk of a bus was warming up with its lights on and lots of people were milling around in its eerie headlights. Art spotted his sister, Chica, first and said, "Wow, what a coincidence! Chica and Rey are going on our same trip!" And he waved to them as he parked the car. Then he spotted our neighbors and he said, "You know, we could have asked them to come with us if we'd only known they were going on the same bus."

Seconds passed, and then there emitted from his pursed lips a steady, low growl as he saw other friends. He shot me a quick, "You didn't!" frown.

I got the same look magnified times 50 when all our friends broke the confetti eggs on top of his head!

And again the same look when the guide/bus owner presented Art with a bottle of tequila and we all had our first toast to the "birthday boy" at 7:00 a.m.

But a smile finally broke through when the group of sixteen from Corpus flashed him with their T-shirts. The white shirts sported a figure that suspiciously looked like Pancho Villa with Art's head; he was sporting a large sombrero, a red bandana, and crossed bandoliers, with a bottle of tequila in one hand and a pistola in the other shooting at a banner that read: "Art Zapata's 50th Birthday Pachanga." The bullet shot out the "50th" and amid the smoke, the "49th" appeared.

They presented a shirt to each of us and that was our uniform of the day! And it was all uphill from there. Great party!

Of course, I had lots of help from our friends, especially Bob Faust, a beer distributor, who brought as a carry-on 50 (not 49?) cases of Miller beer. He stored them in the bus belly until they were safely stored in ours. Obligingly our driver, "Mike," stopped the bus along the side of the highway for us to "refuel" every hour. To some, this was the "Miller highlight" of the trip.

When we entered Monterrey proper, the bus stopped and we welcomed aboard a group of mariachis. As the leader of the musical pack grabbed the microphone, from the back of the bus we heard Ron K. say seriously, "Hi. My name is Carlos. And I'm an alcoholic," and it brought the bus down!

But it all worked! I did it! Art really was surprised! But, then, who wasn't?

****

FISH TALES!

The four or five months before I met Art were chock full of drama. I was rigorously, purposefully changing myself: To begin with, I chose a new career (I arbitrarily decided on court reporting and was pushing myself and my nerves, and had successfully gotten up to 200 words a minute), I acquired two pets (TWO Siamese fighting fish, red and blue, to match my Danish modern furniture) and put them in brandy snifters on the tables attached to the sides of my couch, rejoined my sorority, started a newsletter at work and was successfully fighting off the advances of one of the company's best clients.

I worked in a small engineering office and had for the last two years. I had been assigned to this firm as my first job for Kelley Girls in Fort Lauderdale and while the owner interviewed women for the position of his executive secretary, we became friends and after three weeks, he decided he wanted me for the job. All went well until he hired a bookkeeper (she was lots of fun, loved drinking and ribald talk and I liked her) who eventually started stealing from him. And if that wasn't enough, he also built a lunchroom and hired a cook and beauty operator (she did double-duty) who entertained not only us, as intended, but all of his government clients and, unfortunately, contracted a STD and spread the wealth. To round out the sit-com scenario, the bookkeeper was beaten up by her husband and she sued for divorce. The husband threatened to tell the boss' clients' wives of their escapades, if the bookkeeper pressed charges and continued the divorce proceedings. Oh my!

Now the office was in almost palpable turmoil and I was caught in the middle, just because I had knowledge of everything going on (serves me right for being so nosy). There were lawsuits and subpoenas flying about and I was trying to leave this hazardous environment but the boss kept calling me back.

I was going to court reporting school at night to better myself, to start down a new path and, in the hopes of starting a new life, had applied for a job with a court reporting firm that was managed by a good-looking guy named "Arturo Zapata". He told me at my interview that he had already hired someone for the job but would call me if she didn't pan out. She didn't and he did and I was "in."

It didn't take too long for Art and I to become a couple (several weeks) and on our first date we made it legal and we never again were parted. He never returned to his apartment and we count our first date as our wedding anniversary.

It was on our second date (our zircon anniversary – back then I celebrated by the minute) that he realized what he had signed on for. In an attempt to further woo him, I planned a wonderful tête-à-tête dinner I had never prepared before: Rock cornish game hens and all the trimmings. I set the coffee table with two place settings, added lots of candles and put luxurious pillows around the low table to lounge on while we enjoyed the repast. How romantic!

Following the first two courses, I served the hens. But when he cut into his - HORRORS - there was a package of unmentionable parts that I didn't know were in there but they were cooked to perfection. I told him that they were included to keep it moist, and to just ignore them.

The meal proceeded awkwardly forward but calmed into a great experience until the ending, when Art leaned back to put his drink on the end table next to the sofa. His arm stopped in mid-air, then he shifted his whole body and attention to some object on the table, eyeing it quizzically. "Marilyn, what is this?" And he held up a snifter with a small pile of dust and what seemed to be delicate twigs in the bottom of it.

"Oh, um, er," I stuttered. I was speechless, for there in his hands were the remains of my prized Siamese fighting fish. I spun around to check on the glass on the other table. And, sure enough, it was a matching set and looked the same. I had forgotten to water the fish!

Ashamed, I had to admit to him that what apparently happened was neglect on my part of my watery pets due to the consumption of my time with other pursuits. I then threw myself on the mercy of the court ... reporter.

After a short pause, he made me swear I would never again own another fish nor would I ever forget to take out the bag of edible offal of a fowl (yes, he knew what it was, I had not fooled him). But he forgave me.

However, the fish did not. I imagine when I die and am approaching one of the two gates, I'll be met by the Siamese fighting fish ... and probably the Cornish game hens too ... all of them wanting to settle the score.

****

I DON'T CARE WHAT YOU CALL ME, JUST CALL ME!

When we first moved to Friendswood in 1992, I knew it would take a while to get adjusted and acclimated to a new environment. It was like starting a new life. So, when I found a doctor and filled out all the many forms, when I came to the question that read, "What would you like to be called by the office staff," I wrote down, "Chica." I liked the sound of that (my sister-in-law was nicknamed "Chica" and I always thought it a great "nom de plume"). The next week when I had an appointment with my new dentist, I did the same thing on their paperwork: "Chica." I was now on a roll and when I joined my writer's group, I decided I liked the sound of my pen name being "Chica Zapata," so that's how I introduced myself: "Chica."

"Chica," according to the Urban Dictionary, means: "A name for a girl, preferably an extremely hot girl, that you find pride in just knowing her." I liked that immensely, even if it didn't exactly fit, who would ever know? Also "chica," small "c", could mean girl, small, little or young. Any way you looked at it, I wanted to be called "Chica," and had for years. Even though I was infringing on my sister-in-law's nickname, I figured she would not have any connections with my new contacts, so she would never find out. Plus she always introduced herself as "Ester," her given name, so that would be my defense if ever I needed one.

So I became "Chica" at the doctor's, dentist's and writer's group. It seemed easy enough to have this dual personality, since never the twain shall meet, but over the years my choice of pseudonym (named that for a reason) cost me quite a few embarrassing moments.

At my first dentist's visit, I signed in, and took my seat. I waited a blood-pressure-raising 45 minutes before approaching the little window again. I didn't really want to complain on my first visit, but the nurse kept calling people in to see him that had arrived ten, 20 minutes after I did. To my chagrin, I was told: "Chica, we called your name out many times with no response from anyone, so we figured that you had left the building." Yeah, me and Elvis.

My first doctor's visit was several months later and I had forgotten all about being misnamed. So, as I sat in the waiting room getting madder and madder, instead of listening to the "town crier" more intently, I mainly concentrated on keeping my blood pressure down, since that's what I was there for. Therefore, I missed the call for "Circa Septa" that occurred several times before they stopped calling for her and started looking for "Chacha Zerptra". When I finally worked up my nerve to inquire about how much longer it would be, I was told that the doctor had been called away on an emergency and I would have to reschedule for another time. I was livid. The receptionist then added: "Please, arrive on time for the appointment the next time, since we called your name twice with no response." I went from boiling to blushing in seconds!

I vowed never to miss another call-out from a nurse at either the doctor's or dentist's, and the next visit to the dentist, I rose at the same time as did "Chicha Septtata" and "Sheba Zapta" and got a dirty look from both of them. I stuck my tail between my legs and returned to my seat, only to have to be tapped on the shoulder ten minutes later by the now-knowing nurse in "Nurse Ratchett" guise who had called out "Chica-Chica-Chica" like a cough and who now "tskked" and "tskked" all the way down the hallway as she led me to my appointed room where I would meet the doctor, whatever his name was.

But my writing class was different. I kept rapt attention and only one time did I miss getting "Chica's" corrected paper and had to retrieve it with a red face. But after the semester was over, three of us remained in touch and decided to meet once a month (therein lies the problem) and critique each other's stories. I figured with only two people besides me in attendance, we'd be sitting close together, so, at best, I had a one-out-of-three chance of getting my name right. There was no way in hell I could forget who I was the next time.

Not so. At our first get-together I fell off the wagon. I read my short story that I had written and laid my paper down ready to receive the good and the bad. "Nice job, Chica," they both said cheerily in unison. And I turned around to look for my sister-in-law.

****

THE WOLF IN THE WIND!

In 1982, wanting to go as far as we could go in the Arctic Circle before we had to call it quits, we flew over the MacKenzie Deltas to Tuktoyaktuk, Northwest Territories, a small hamlet of 300 cold souls on the shores of the Arctic Ocean, just 100 miles south of the permanent polar ice cap.

Boarding the small charter flight on Kenn Borek Air, Limited, was an adventure in itself. The seating ratio was half-and-half - half passengers and half strapped-down liquor. Passengers to the right and liquor to the left (the bottles were safety-belted in better than we were).

Out of the window, I spotted two Inuit women boarding the small plane in fantastic fur-lined coats. When they were finally seated, I approached them and asked where they were purchased their "anoraks." Fortunately, they both bought them in "Tuk" from a little old lady in a trailer (who only sewed on Sundays, I bet). I knew my mission and quest. Never again would I be cold during the freezing Northern Indiana winters, snow up to the eaves with Civil Defense and tanks on the road in front of the house for "just in cases."

So, that was how we finally arrived at "as far as

we can go." It may not have been the end of the world, but you could see it from there. And it was beautiful and barren and brutal.

I read that this was a place of bone-carvers, but found it was no more. When a large oil company moved in, the Inuits still possessing this skill had opted instead for the big salaries and left their craft. But not wanting to take "No" for an answer to any question, I talked Art into visiting about a dozen houses before happening upon the coat-maker wife and bone-carver husband. A match made in heaven. There was a pile of reindeer bones and antlers beside their trailer steps, and after we got to know the two artists better, they said to take all I wanted. I did. Some days you're just damn lucky.

Upon entering the cluttered trailer of the local seamstress, I knew we came to the right place. Bones, antlers, pelts and beautiful wolf and fox tails were scattered about on the few pieces of furniture. She showed me the coats that were available for sale, but there was only one that howled my name: A blue wool undercoat with fur-lined hood, a long bushy Arctic wolf tail hung down the back, and fur covered the hem. This "first coat" was accompanied by a "second coat," a poplin insulated overcoat with embroidered dog sleds and malamute teams circling the hem. As an added touch, she had also sewn two wolf paws with claws onto the collar of the blue wool, so they would hang down the front of the coat. It was utterly breath-taking! I tried to bargain for a better price, but she was up to the task and said $300 was as low as she could go. So be it. I had to have it. I raised my fist and swore, "As 'Ullr' is my witness, I'll never be cold again!" (Ullr is the Norse god of snow.)

Her husband only had one artistic carving left. It was a caribou bone carving of an Inuit killing a large bird on the ice with a club. How did he know that was just what I wanted?

While I was in the throes of packing up my purchases with the husband, Art chatted with the woman of the trailer and I eavesdropped on their exchange.

"So, how do you like living in "Tuk"?

"Not so much."

"How come?"

"Too many people!" An odd comment, I thought, to describe a town of 300 residents scattered over such a large expanse.

Art persisted: "So, where would you like to live?"

"I want to go back home."

"Where is that?"

"Up north!" Had she really said she wanted to go up north?

I could stand it no more. I said, "NORTH!!? We are north! There is very little north left! If we go farther north, it would be south!"

And she laughed, humoring her customer.

****

Postscript: I wore my fantastic coveted coat only once in my lifetime, on the streets of South Bend, Indiana. As I strolled one blustering snowy day down the city streets, I felt all warm and toasty. But it's windy in South Bend and as I turned the corner, a gust roaring between the buildings hit me full frontal. The wolf paws started to move and then began swinging wildly. They were slapping me upside the face and landing down on my chest. Then claws drawn, they'd sweep across my face, then box my ears. I was screaming Jack London's name in vain. As I ran for cover, the wolf's paws were swept high above my head, frantically clawing at the sky in an attempt to break free. Upon reaching sanctuary in a building lobby, the pelt started settling down. I asked the receptionist for the location of the nearest bathroom and also for some duct tape. Once there, I cleaned up the scratches and wiped off my blood, then taped the paws to the coat before I ventured back out into the wild. I never wore the animal again!

Double Postscript: Three weeks after my adventure on the streets of South Bend, at our annual Christmas party, we announced Art had accepted a federal job in Corpus Christi, Texas! I thought my friends would bemoan our leaving, but my tennis partner turned to the woman sitting next to her and said, "Will you be my new partner?" So off we drove, pulling our boatload of snow (not on purpose but we didn't know how to get rid of it) that lasted until Kansas, heading to a place where wolf coats were kept in storage and the temperatures reached 100 on a cool day. A few years later my Arctic woolen treasure was donated to and adopted by the Houston Community College Drama Department and today lives a quiet life in a locker waiting for the day the powers that be decide to present "Dr. Zhivago" as their production.

****

EMULATING MARILYN!

In 1970, much to my consternation, regret and embarrassment, my first husband/second-to-last husband was in a courtroom filing for a divorce from me. Unfortunately, this was a time before "no-fault" divorces and one had to be processed through the adversarial system, meaning that a divorce could be obtained only through a showing of fault of "ONE" of the parties in a marriage. This had to be something more than not loving one another; it meant that one spouse had to plead that the other had committed adultery, abandonment, felony, or other similarly culpable acts. In other words, there had to be a "valid reason" for severing the marriage ties.

My attorney had wisely advised that I not attend this hearing since there were going to be many hurtful things said about me. I knew I was not guilty of any of the above-mentioned acts, but I took his advice, then later begged him for the gory details. I wish I hadn't asked.

It would have been humorous, if it hadn't been happening to me, but my ex's number-one reason for divorcing all centered around food. He threw himself on the mercy of the court by whining about the cruel and unusual punishment I had bestowed upon him by culinarily depriving him of nourishment. I should have gone with the adultery and abandonment ... or, best of all, the felony.

His pitiful plea for justice was broken down into several categories, the first being: One time I used my weekly allowance for food (yes, Archie Bunker, them were the days) and bought a mirror for the entryway. In my defense (which I would have used for the court but instead am relaying to you), my reasoning was that the food would be eaten and flushed and the mirror would be something we would possess happily ever after (the statement was true except for the "we"). My attorney told me my "ex" told the judge: "I use it now to watch my face as my cheeks sink in and my body shrinks." As it turns out 45 years later, that purchase was a brilliant move on my part. I no longer have that husband, nor does anyone since he died years ago, not from hunger, I presume (if this sounds bitter, I'm doing my job right). But I still have the mirror in my "real" husband's and my garage used daily for a quick check of my lipstick and Cheshire smile as I leave saying, with satisfaction, "I told you so." Plus I have fodder for a chapter in this book.

His second whine was about the time I bought a roast and fried it since I was in a hurry. The only part that was edible was the middle and that was for only one meal when it was intended for three. I was out of money (due to a mosaic lamp still viable in my "real" mother-in-law's yard), so when I packed his lunch the next day, I made him a "burnt fat/charred jerky" sandwich. When he complained that he was the laughing stock of the office when he opened his lunch, I thought I'd make him even more popular and the next day sent him a "bone" sandwich. Again in my defense, if I had gotten to use it: I got caught up on making money and meals come out even and I got a good giggle out of it as did his mates. But some people have no sense of humor, especially if they're hungry.

The **pièce de résistance** of his complaints he saved for last. I was told he almost sobbed to the judge: "She feeds me colored foods." Even the judicial personage was taken aback and asked for a clarification. He continued: "So far she's served me green mashed potatoes for St. Patrick's Day, purple pasta for Mardi Gras, blue potato salad for Easter, yellow and orange bread for Halloween, red rice for Christmas, turquoise pancakes and pink alphabet soup! I rest my case."

My defense would have been: "Well, Marilyn Monroe's favorite dish that she ate regularly and served to Joe were green peas and carrots just because they were pretty. Jayne Mansfield dyed her poodle to match her clothes, especially pink. (I copied this one too since I had several white cats who celebrated fur-colored holidays with me for years.) I guess I like color in my life."

Needless to say, the judge wholeheartedly agreed with the petitioner and dissolved our marriage on those nebulous grounds forthwith.

Now, in 2016, I recently read in The Houston Chronicle about a new chef in Washington, D.C., who was drawing big crowds to his restaurant and receiving rave reviews. He specialized in coloring foods to make them more exciting and enticing. I rest **MY** case.

****

STREETWALKER!

1972 was the dawning of the age of freedom for women, so not only did I smoke, but I also subscribed to Cosmopolitan, went into bars alone at night and considered it "business wear" to go to work in one of my two polyester hot-pants suits, the coats barely covering the hem of my short pants. I dyed my hair a bright red and wore it very long with the obligatory bangs, backcombed it furiously on top to make me two inches taller, with an elaborate pony tail dangling down my right shoulder, the end curling gently over my right breast.

In the first half of my tenure of two years working for an engineering firm in Ft. Lauderdale, Florida, it was my habit that once a week, I would tack an extra half-hour onto my lunch hour and walk the short three blocks to downtown to have my hair done.

On the first really warm day in April of that year, the sun was shining brightly as I returned from the salon with an exceptionally high "do". I was feeling hot in more ways than one. Wanda, my hair-dresser had done a great job that day and the Florida sun sparkled off the red in my tresses as I traipsed back to the office. The walking wasn't particularly easy, since along with my hot-pants, I'd also worn my lace-up Roman sandals.   Quite a sight!

When I was within a block of our offices, I first felt, then heard, then noticed a car driving slowly up behind me and as it came up even with me, the driver gave me the "look." Our eyes locked and he raised his eyebrows, opening his eyes wide, smiled a crooked smile and nodded his head slightly as he cruised past me. I watched as the car proceeded down the street with the driver constantly repositioning his rear-view mirror so he could get a longer look, then he slowed the car even more and parallel parked into a metered parking spot about a block from me, almost in front of the engineering office where I toiled.

A dapper man in casual clothes got out of the car, then leaned against the meter and turned his attention completely on me as I sauntered in his direction.

It must have gone to my head, and I remember thinking, "Boy, I must look really hot this afternoon," and without meaning to, started to -- I can only describe it as "strut my stuff" in his direction.

At that moment, ANOTHER car came rolling past me with the driver, a few years older than the first, also giving me the "come on," even going so far as to actually whistle and wave. Then he abruptly turned the corner in front of me, parked in a no-parking zone and was waiting for me at the stop light. I was only three stores away from him but my heart raced those last few yards before we met. How exciting this was, I thought, "I'm glad I tipped Wanda that extra fifty cents, it's sure worth it."

"Hey, Gorgeous, you're the best thing that's happened to me all day." That's a direct quote from the driver (indelibly remembered after all these years) as he greeted me, actually tipping his Captain hat (as in "The Captain and Tenille") in my direction. I beamed.

"My name is Gary and I feel like I've met you before. What's your name?"

"Marilyn," I said shyly.

"How about you and me having some fun?"

"I don't know," I said. My mind was reeling. I didn't want to answer too fast, but I knew I really had no plans that evening except to watch "Dallas," but I'd readily give up J.R. for this "Gary guy" and a free meal, hopefully shrimp. Maybe even steak at Joe Namath's place ... from the looks of his sporty car.

"Aw, come on! We could have a great time! How about the beach or a movie? I've got the afternoon free."

"No, I guess not." I had been hoping he was talking about the evening, but I knew I had to get back to work, and had only a few minutes to spare. I guess I could give him my phone number for another time if he asks.

"Why not? I've got the money, Honey, and you've got the time!"

"No, I don't. I'm really sorry. I can't. I've got to get back to work. I'm a secretary at that place down the street," and I pointed to the white office building. And then I remembered the man down the street waiting for me. After all, this one was pushy and rushing me, but the other one was patiently waiting for me. Even at this distance, I thought I liked him better. And after all, he did get first dibs. I can pick and choose. How popular can I get? I thought conceitedly.

Then it seemed that Gary lost his bright approach. He said: "I'm sorry to bother you, ma'am. I really am. I'm working under cover for the Ft. Lauderdale Police Department. And there has been a load of complaints about prostitution downtown here. And I thought, er ... I'm really sorry."

That sound I heard was my bubble bursting. I was speechless. But he wasn't, he went on. "And, please, my apologies also for my partner," and he pointed to the cute guy waiting for me down the street, "we're just trying to do our job. No harm, no foul. Have a nice day." And off he went.

He waved to his partner who stamped out his cigarette, got in his car and left. So did Gary ... and my visions of shrimp and any semblance of self-worth I might have had.

Along with my ego, I think my hair sagged an inch after this encounter. Definitely my strut receded. And my stomach growled.

****

SENIORS SAY THE DARNDEST THINGS!

The topic of conversation around the restaurant table between the four of us, the Spencers and the Zapatas, was all about our maladies, despite my warning that we would never be so old to talk about regularity at the dinner table. After Art, Norma and I had stated our latest body part to go awry, it was Charlie's turn. He said: "I'm really doing fine, except for the fact that I hurt all over. That's why I wouldn't know I had a symptom if I had one!"

****

We were on a road trip to old haunts where we used to live, and I stopped in to visit a friend who I hadn't seen in quite a while. She was getting ready to go grocery shopping. I said I could take her and bring her back, since it was only a few miles from her home. She said she didn't shop at that one any more because it was to the north and now she only could go east and west, and swore never to go north and south again. I asked if that didn't make it difficult for her. She said, "Not really, besides my grocery store, I only had to change my lawyer, my church, my bank, my pharmacy, my doctor, my bowling alley, my dentist, but I do kind of miss seeing my sister!"

41

Once when we were visiting my folks in Wichita, I went out to the farm to visit another cousin, Kathleen, who was ailing. Alicia Zenner, my cousin's daughter, was there taking care of her and greeted us when we came in and led us into the living room where her mother was watching TV. Kathleen was in her robe, sitting in a recliner, and was attached to an oxygen tank. I said hello and pulled a chair up in front of her and began to catch her up with all my news. After fifteen minutes of my diatribe, she started to look faint and gasping for breath. I turned to Alicia and said, "Maybe we should leave so she can get some rest." Alicia said, "That would be all right, but it's a better idea if you would, please, just move your chair off of the oxygen tube; you're cutting off her air."

****

Betsy and Jeff Miller went to San Miguel with us for a week. We had a fabulous time showing them around, the good (pyramid/upscale restaurants/spa/market), bad (bullfight/downscale restaurants) and the ugly (we could find nothing to fit this category). One night we decided on a "fun" downscale restaurant for dinner located on the second floor of what was rumored to be an old brothel. The waitress came to take our order after we found our own well-worn seats around a rickety old table (but there was a great view out the window). "What'll you have?" the waitress asked through the cigarette she had clamped in her mouth. Betsy said, "The shrimp." The waitress frowned and said, "I wouldn't recommend it," (The Gulf was a long ways away), and she waited poised with her pad for Betsy's order. Betsy said, "You know, I really feel like shrimp tonight." We offered to go to another restaurant for shrimp. "I'm sorry, but I think the shrimp is bad," the puzzled waitress repeated. So, I ordered tacos, Art ordered enchiladas, Jeff ordered fajitas, and we all turned toward Betsy, "I'll have the shrimp, please," she said politely.

That night Montezuma visited and said he agreed with the waitress, "Bad shrimp."

****

My tennis club of 50 women, mostly over the age of 60, had a birthday party and everyone was invited for a little tennis tournament and a potluck lunch afterwards. We finished our matches at noon and got ready to go dine. The sound was deafening to our ears .... "KRRRRIIIIPPPP" ... as everyone tore off their elbow bands, wrist bands, knee braces, ankle wraps and arm wraps.

We were thereby dubbed "The Velcro Gang."

****

Edwina just got back from Hungary and the "old country." She went on a cruise down the Danube and it was windy whenever she went ashore. On her return home, she ruminated on her experience and made a succinct observation: If you wore a scarf on your head and tied it in back, you were treated like a foreigner, but if you wore it over your head and tied it under your chin, they spoke to you in another language.

Bet they also have a different word for everything.

****

Meena and Randy Sinha had just returned from a river cruise tour. They told of a woman on their trip who, before lunch one day, came running into the dining room and announced she had lost her passport and her cash had been stolen. She couldn't remember where she had last seen either, but she was almost sure she had had both things in her hands that morning as they left on a city tour. Of course, she was all atwitter and panicky, but the tour guide said all would be well. He found a substitute guide to lead them on the scheduled tour he had planned for that afternoon and he and the elderly lady who lost her passport went to the American Embassy to report the loss and get a temporary replacement. The substitute guide got a phone call when the group stopped for dinner. The guide and misguided lady had arrived at the Embassy and, since the line was long, the woman had excused herself to the restroom. She came out red-faced. She embarrassingly had to confess her "senior moment." When she had pulled down her trousers for her restroom visit, she discovered that she had tucked her passport and money into her panty hose for safekeeping. And safe and hidden it was from everyone including her.

On the bright side, she will never need to buy rouge again!

****

The message on my friend and neighbor, Barbara Ladd's answering machine: "I'm away from the phone right now. I'll call you back as soon as I return or as soon as I can find the phone.

****

After a Renaissance-themed party at our house, our neighbor, Sheri Boren, went home early and found she had forgotten to feed her dog. She did so then much to his ecstatic gratefulness. She then went to Walmart for late grocery shopping causing quite a curious stir, and in the parking lot a police officer eyed her warily. It was only when she got home and looked in the mirror that she discovered that she was still wearing her elaborately-jeweled, plastic crown that I had bestowed on everyone's Medieval head.

Heavy weighs the crown!

****

For Houstonians: After I overheard a young lady at Cato's clothes store talking about how her mother was dating a younger man, I decided to share and told her I was a cougar. She looked at me and grinned and said, "I am too. I'm a senior. What was your major?"

Where's my walker?

****

A tennis friend, Cindy Dalene, told me that her mother had a blepharoplasty procedure done on her eyes. I admitted to her that I'd had the same thing done to mine years earlier, since all of my life I'd had too much skin folded in my lids, and my insurance finally agreed with me. It was the best thing that ever happened to my face, I could see in all directions without turning my head, and it was glorious. I asked Cindy if her mother was pleased with the results.

She said her mother called her two weeks after the operation and asked, "How long have we had ceiling fans in the bedroom?"

****

I was just thinking: I bit my lip the other day. Wouldn't you think that after 73 years of practice my lip would learn to get out of the way of the teeth? What a slacker. My body parts are getting dumber and dumber.

****

Paula's mother would never eat eggs and chicken together (like on a salad). She said it was too incestuous to eat.

****

We went to an Alzheimer's seminar (mainly for the meal and, like in Playboy, to read the articles) and a woman there explained that she was attending the talk because the disease ran rife in her family (welcome to my club) and that even her memory foam mattress was having trouble remembering its shape.

****

MORE THAN DOUBLE FAULTS!

DOG DAY AFTERNOON!

My Friendswood tennis team was playing Monday League tennis outdoors in a new location ... for us ... in Houston. Wafting over the heat waves of Texas came a delicious smell. My partner, Pat Bevan, and I were in the first set and on a changeover we debated about where to go for lunch. The saliva-inducing breeze seemed to be coming from nearby, so we mentioned it to our opponents and asked where that restaurant was. They hemmed and hawed and said they didn't know. We raised our eyebrows, then rackets, and buckled down and beat them for not sharing their private cafe ... we guessed that that was the reason they wouldn't divulge its whereabouts.

Pat and I watched the rest of our team's matches and when all had finished, we suggested to the group that we should go for lunch to the nearby restaurant since it smelled like the BBQ was wonderful. Everyone was starved having played two hours with that enticing smell hovering over the courts, and everyone readily agreed on our choice.

Since no one had been able to learn the whereabouts of this restaurant (several other girls asked their opponents like we did with no response - we figured they were mad since we beat them and didn't want us to join them at "their" favorite place to eat after tennis), we asked the receptionist at the clubhouse desk where that fabulous smell was coming from and the girl seemed embarrassed.

Upon much begging and pressing by us, she reluctantly revealed that the club was located near an animal clinic that had a crematorium that operated once a week on Mondays.

Instant appetite loss and celebration buzz kill. We all went home victorious but hungry that day.

****

GET WELL QUICK, VANDA!

I thought it odd when Pearlie Renken sent out an email to all our tennis friends saying not to send Vanda Gemelli any more emails since she had a virus, but I respected her wishes, and took Vanda's name off of my sub list when I sent out a request for someone to take my place.

The next day at the tennis club, I saw Vanda on the court playing in a tough match. Since I was playing on the court next to her, when we changed sides, I rushed over to check on how she was doing in her unhealthy state and whether she had miraculously recovered from the flu overnight.

She was taken aback and didn't know what I was talking about until I explained to her about Pearlie's email. She started laughing and I thought, "What a great recovery ... I want some of that medicine!"

Then she explained that the virus was in her computer and not in her. Again the SMAs (Senior Moment Adventures) had struck gold.

****

THINGS I'LL NEVER FORGET - LIKE RIDING A BIKE!

When I was anticipating one of my various and sundry operations, the doctor advised me to do exercises on a stationary bike in order to build up the muscles in and around the soon-to-be replaced knees.

I had recently resurrected my bike from childhood with the fat seat and thin blow-up tires but had painted it and named it and now it was only an art piece. Also I no longer had my stationary bike that I used to keep in the bedroom. For the last few years of my possession of it, it was filling the role of wig holder and, since I'm a good multi-tasker, I had bracelets lining the handlebars and clothes draping over the seat and fender, until one day Art drew a halt to having this obscene creature in his sleeping area. He said to get rid of it. I knew a garage sale was not the answer, since at almost every sale I've had the privilege of attending, right at the end of the driveway will sit a barely used, shiny metal sculpture known as the "obligatory piece of exercise equipment."

I decided to give the bike away to someone who would give it a good home, so I sent out an email to friends saying it could be theirs for the taking, with the one caveat being, as suggested by Art, that it was theirs permanently, first come/first served, but like a tennis ace, it could never be returned. And so it came to pass that a friend was willing to adopt it, in fact eager to use it, and Art delivered the awkward monstrosity to her forthwith.

Fast forward to my pending surgery and advice from the doctor that I needed to use a like bike. Reluctant to buy another one, I called Tana Burton and said, "I know that Art promised that it could never be returned, but I'm wondering if you'd be willing to let me be an Indian giver and take my stationary bike back." She was more than happy, she said, to get rid of it as she never used it any more and had relegated it upstairs to the guest bedroom. But her husband was away on a week-long business trip and wouldn't be there to take it down from upstairs and bring it over, but we were welcome to come and pick it up if I needed it right away.

She lived only blocks away from us, so I coerced Art into going back to pick it up and he didn't say a word, ostensibly since I really needed it for health reasons. So we went to Tana's and she had her kids drag the thing downstairs and Art loaded the unwieldy recumbent bike into the van with only unsaid swear words written all over his face. I profusely thanked Tana for giving it back and she said, "No problem. Good riddance."

When we got home the first thing I did was spend a half hour on the wheel while watching, appropriately, Wheel of Fortune. The time went by fast and smoothly, much more smoothly than I remembered, and I vowed to use it every day.

After I finished I got up and went to the computer to check emails. There were many offers from my tennis friends to come get their long-neglected exercise machines, but the one that caught my eye was the one from Norma. She wrote, "Although Art made me promise I wouldn't give your bike back ... I hope it's all right with him ... you're welcome to it. I am wanting to buy a recumbent bike since they are lots better even if they're more expensive. So come and get it!"

I sat staring at the screen for a while. "Recumbent." That was the key word. At one time I had owned a recumbent bike but it wasn't stationary ... or was it? I called Art at the office to pick his memory of our bike. He too had thought something was funny when he loaded it into the van. He said, "You know, of course it's not your bike. Now I do remember that yours wasn't a recumbent and that I delivered it to Charlie and Norma's and even made her sign a fake legal paper that she would never return it!"

Immediately I hung up and called Tana. "Oh, my God," she said. "I'm so glad you called. Tommy got home last night and packed his suitcase away in the spare bedroom closet. When he came downstairs he said, 'What happened to that expensive bike I got you last Christmas that you said you couldn't live without?' I told him you borrowed it for a little while before your surgery and that you were going to bring it back. I hope you don't hold it against me for being a double-Indian giver, but when you said you gave it to me, I believed you! I'm so, so sorry!"

So was I. I really liked that bike much better than mine. But all's well that ends well. Norma got to keep the bike I gave her. I got to use a Cadillac stationary bike and strengthened my knees so surgery was a breeze. Tana got Tommy's gift back and started to use it again and lost 20 pounds. Everyone was happy except Art. He had to load up the metal monster and take it back to Tana but he said he was more than eager to do it one more time, but never wanted a stationary bike to darken our doors again. Luckily he didn't mention treadmills, stair-steppers or weight-lifting sets, since I'm starting to get a hankering for one of those because my bracelet collection is overflowing on the old standing light poles.

****

SACKING TENNIS FRIENDS!

After a botched blepharoplasty (if it's any help, I also had to look it up, it's a cosmetic eye surgery for those flaps of skin on the eyelids that grow with age and threaten to block out the whole world), I refused to let anybody see me. When friends would come a'calling, I would place a brown paper bag over my head and talk to them through the air holes I made in it.

As more and more visitors arrived, I elaborated on the bag. I drew eyes on it and glued on fake eyelashes. I painted a nose and mouth and put little holes in them. Then I pierced the bag and hung earrings on the sides. Lots of swirling feathered yarn adorned the top of the bag. I felt I looked "reasonably attractive" with "reasonably" being a much misused word.

Some people like Pat Bevan and Joan Hughes found it difficult to talk to me, when they had to stare at me sipping a margarita through a straw with a sack over my head. But within two weeks, I was at least semi-acceptable visually to go out in public and not fear frightening babies and dogs any more than usual. But it was weeks before I returned to the tennis courts.

I planned the day of my comeback to coincide with a day of league play when many of my friends would be at the clubhouse. I decided to come early and get in some "conversating". As I rounded the corner of the entryway, I broke down in laughter and tears ... well, maybe just laughter. There sat about a dozen women on a tiered bleacher, all with sacks over their heads that were painted with various faces, all featuring plenty of eyeshadow, mascara, blush and lipstick, plastered across the front of the brown masks, some with only HEB as a decoration and some with immensely large air holes. It warmed me cockles and I vowed never to quit the racket and these friends.

****

IT HAPPENS TO EVERYONE!

From Mary Jean Grammens, a Chancellor's Tennis Player:

I saw Judy Tran in Sam's Club and we stood talking and catching up for about a half hour. During that time a little bug was flying around my face. Several times I took off my glasses to see if they needed cleaning and then passed my hand around my face trying to scare away the bug. Judy, at one time, even said she saw it and tried to catch it for me, also with no luck.

When I got home and still saw the bug, it finally dawned on me that I had a floater in my eye. I had never had one before but my husband, Rich, always talked about his and he said it was exactly like he experienced. Later, this diagnosis was confirmed when I went to the ophthalmologist for my pre-op cataract surgery exam.

I'd have rather had a friendly gnat adopt me!

****

INVITING TEAM!

When we lived in Portland, Texas, I threw my tennis team an end-of-the-season party. I sent out invitations by taking a fresh flour tortilla, folding it over and adding chopped crepe paper in the shape of orange cheese strips, white onions slices, red peppers and green pickles, then enclosing a printed invite cut like a hamburger patty with brown, singed edges. It was a beautiful work of art and everyone commented on how clever I was and I felt a little like Edison.

Then we moved to Friendswood and about ten years later, I threw my new tennis team an end-of-the-season party and remembered the tortilla invitation, and figured it was time to bring it out of storage and use it once more. Again, everyone commented on how cute and original it was and I was proud of my invention.

About a year later, I got a call from Janie Mitchell, a friend who had left our Houston team and moved to Corpus Christi. She had joined a tennis club there and made some new friends. She said that at their end-of-season party, she and her partner were talking about their old tennis partners. Her new friend said she had a wild and crazy partner many years earlier who threw an end-of-season party and sent out real tortilla invitations. Janie had a good laugh at that and then said, "I've also got a crazy friend who did the same thing but she said it was her own idea and that she made it up herself. I can't wait to call her on it and get on her case for plagiarism." The friend asked Janie, "What's her name?" I can only imagine their laughter at discovering they shared a friend in me.

When we finally put the puzzle together, I know I for one was thrilled at being exonerated from having stolen the idea, and I realized there was no non-patent infringement by another "crazy person".

****

PREMATURE CONDOLENCES!

As we got on the tennis court, Bobbie Myers told me an old tennis friend of ours, Debbie, had lost her husband a few days earlier. I pictured sweet Debbie Zendt in my mind and thought: She's so nice and has young children. How was she going to manage? We've got to do something nice for her.

A day later while shopping in Sports Authority, I turned down the women's tennis shoe aisle and there stood Debbie. I ran up to her and put my arms around her. "Oh, Debbie, I'm so sorry to hear about your husband," I gushed.

She looked at me quizzically and asked, "What about him?"

"Um ... you know ... that he .... died." I stammered through that sentence.

She laughed (what a cold hearted bitch, I thought) and said, "Well, he seemed all right this morning when I kissed him goodbye to go play tennis! What do you know that I don't?"

I just stared at her. And we broke out laughing.

I called Bobbie when I got home and she explained that it was another Debbie that I didn't even know whose husband had died, but that all their children were grown and also had children and he had been sick for a while, so it was expected. I told her that I had seen Debbie Zendt shopping and said I was so sorry about her husband.

Bobbie said, "What? Did he die too? I've got to let the others know so we can do something."

It took a while before we got the whole thing straightened out in our minds (I think), but Debbie did tell me later that someone inexplicably brought over food that night and just left it on the porch and she couldn't figure out why until I sent her this story!

****

LET ME IN OR ELSE I'LL CALL THE POLICE!

When we moved from Portland, we rented a home (a whole other story) in Shore Acres, a suburb of Houston. To open a bank account, we opted for Bank of America since it has locations all over and we surely would find one near our new home-to-be. The one we would use until then was located across from NASA and had a crazy setup. The bank proper was in a self-standing building with tellers and safety deposit boxes. But their drive-through was located about a block away down the street.

One day after tennis I was going home and had planned on stopping at the bank to put something in our safety deposit box. It was 1:00 on a Friday and I knew they were open, there were lots of cars out in the parking lot. I climbed the high stairs to the front door and saw lots of people inside. I tried to open the door but it was locked. I banged on the door but nobody acknowledged me. I banged harder. Still no response.

So I moved down to another door, also locked. I banged and banged and banged until my hands were blue in the face. I was so pissed I couldn't stand it. Nobody, but nobody even looked my way and I KNEW they heard me.

I ran to my car and drove hell-bent over to the drive-through. Luckily there was no line. I rolled down my window (yes, it was that long ago) and looked angrily at the girl. "I have been banging on the door to the bank and nobody ... NOBODY ... would let me in. I have something to put in my safety deposit box and there are people in there and there's no reason why they shouldn't open the door and let me in! What are you going to do about it?"

"I'm sorry, ma'am. But I do know why they wouldn't let you in."

"What is it?" I demanded.

"The bank is being robbed and the police are on their way!"

****

FRITOS CRAVING!

On my way home after a particularly strenuous tennis match, I could hardly wait to get home to get cleaned up, eat and take a nap. I took off my tennis shoes and wet T-shirt and changed in the car before I started driving. I looked at the clock and it was after 1:00 p.m. and I still hadn't had a thing to eat. I had a sudden craving for some Fritos. I didn't even know if I could make it home, the desire was so great, but I hung in there and drove the 45 minutes home thinking only of nachos for lunch.

When I got home, I tossed my clothes in the closet hamper and dropped my shoes and socks on the floor. Grabbing my robe, I wrapped it around me, went to the kitchen and made me some of the best nachos ever. It was only later when I revisited my closet that I realized that my shoes smelled, nay reeked, which I had mistaken for Fritos. I'll probably never eat corn chips again!

(In telling this stories to my editors, they said their feet don't smell like Fritos. That's news to me. Mine have smelled that way ever since I first used that sense, and I thought everybody's did!)

****

BUFFALO BILL GATES!

Some of my tennis friends have a harder time than others accepting and learning new things to keep up technologically in the 21st Century. But gradually we're all getting on line. Since we set our matches months in advance, it's important that we all keep "in the loop" and make sure we're all on the same page, just in case someone can't make a match, needs to get a sub, or to let people know whether you'll be late or not.

One day a friend of mine, Emma, showed up an hour early for our match. Albeit she's in her seventies, but then who isn't at this club? Anyway, she recently got her first computer and was just learning in bytes and pieces. When I finally arrived for our tennis game, she explained her predicament, about having to wait an extra hour. I asked her why she didn't check her emails the day before to find the email I sent with the time change.

Her response was: "Because I didn't turn my computer on. I didn't think they delivered emails on Sunday!"

****

DRUNKEN BINOCULARS!

We needed tequila - who doesn't? But we did officially since we were planning a party at our house, hosting a couple I intended to cultivate as our first non-family Mexican friends.

As usual, I was in a hurry and, after gathering up several bottles off the shelves at the liquor store, approached the counter, only to find I was behind a woman who apparently was cultivating a small country as her friends. From her cart, she plopped four gallon-bottles onto the counter in front of the register, then took out three pairs of binoculars and placed them alongside the bottles.

The clerk rang up the binoculars at $9.99 each. Cheap, I thought! But why would she buy them in a liquor store? Not given to shyness, I decided to approach this happy stranger and perhaps hear an interesting story in my downtime in line. All I said was: "Why?"

She explained that she and her husband were going on a cruise with two other couples, and since it was impossible to smuggle liquor bottles on board, they were going to try this method. The plastic binoculars were flasks with all the bells, whistles and moving parts of a real pair! Of course, I just had to have one!

That evening, I proudly showed Art my purchase! He smirked and said, "What the hell do you want with those for?" I lapsed into the liquor store tale. He said, "But we don't cruise. Never have, never will. You know I get seasick. And you've always said cruising on the open sea was boring. What a waste of a good ten dollars!"

Two days later, he revealed his plan. He had signed us up for a two-week river cruise down the Blue Danube, to leave in 45 days. Best $9.99 I ever spent.

But wait, there's more!

On the cruise, I told this story. Everybody within earshot wanted a pair for themselves. At the end of our trip, I gave my empty flask to our new best friends, a couple from Mexico (our second non-family Mexican friends). They were grateful and couldn't wait to share their story with friends (we were their first non-family Texan friends).

Several years later, on a dreary Monday in January, we received a package in the mail. Inside was a touching letter from the wife of our favorite shipmates informing us that her husband had succumbed to pancreatic cancer the month before. But she was writing to let us know that they had carried the flask that I had given them on two more cruises before he was felled by his disease, and they always talked of joining us in Texas to relive our adventures together. She was sad that they never had the chance to visit us in Texas, but wondered if it would be all right if her daughter could visit us on her upcoming trip to Houston. How exciting? Of course, we wanted to meet her.

On the day of her welcome to Texas party, I hurried to the liquor store to supplement my supply of wine. While in line, I noticed a woman emptying her cart onto the counter: Superior tequila, a blue liqueur, four pairs of red-white-and-blue feathered handcuffs, a pair of binoculars, and a corkscrew attached to a calf's hoof.

Of course, I asked her to the party!

****

BORROWED HOUSES!

In May 1991, Art, my husband, and I moved to Houston from Corpus Christi, Texas. For four months we lived in a rented house, after answering an unbelievable ad in the newspaper: "Live in a 3,000-plus square foot luxury home for only $200 a month." This rental company, Show Homes of America, handled problem homes, homes that were hard to sell for whatever reason, and matched them to renters with furniture and decorations to complement the house to help it sell.

After viewing photographs of our "stuff," we were assigned to a structure in Shore Acres, a small suburb near the water, that was exceptionally eclectic (no offense intended, I'm sure). Each room was a square module connected haphazardly to the main core of the house that had a wide hallway fit for a nursing home. From the sky the configuration must have resembled a DNA chain. We loved it.

The program was perfect for our needs. We didn't have to put our belongings and furniture in storage, plus we had time to search for a Houston suburb to our liking where we would buy our "real home."

This DNA house had been on the market for two years but in the four months we called it "home," there was quite a bit of traffic of prospective buyers entering through its many portals, enough so that a few days before we left on vacation, I dutifully called the house manager: "We're going to Venezuela on vacation for a few weeks. Be sure to lock the door if the house is shown."

"Didn't you get the Certified Letter?"

"No. What letter?"

"The house sold. Hallelujah! You guys are great. But we have to get you into another house before the new owners move in next week."

"NEXT WEEK! But we're leaving in two days."

"No problem," she said cheerfully, "we have lots of houses for you!"

An hour after I hung up the phone, we met her in Friendswood, our city of choice, at a house comprising 4,500 square feet. She warned, "If you want this one, you'll need more furniture for the third living room."

Blinded by its beauty and spaciousness, we excitedly said: "We do want it. The extra furniture is no problem." Were we out of our minds?

A half hour later, we were at Star Furniture buying a massive white sectional sofa and two large matching chaise lounges to be delivered the next day.

When we finally returned to Shore Acres that evening, we called some movers I found in the local Green Sheet who promised to arrive at 7:00 a.m. the next morning and move all we had for a set fee of $1,000 sight-unseen.

"But we've got lots of stuff!" I warned.

"Is no problem. We move all."

We packed frantically though the night.

The next morning, in a sleep-deprived daze, we realized the movers were late. Leaving Art to finish packing, I scoured the neighborhood in my car and spotted a large moving van listing to one side, with a load of flattened paper boxes tied to the roof and one turbaned man riding the floorboard. I approached the van which held two Indians (not from the Wild West but from India) inside and asked if they were looking for me.

"Oh, yes, Miss." I liked them already.

They followed me home, almost running into the ditch but overcorrecting and taking out the lower branches of the trees in front of our house.

As they entered the living room, they pointed out a few "exceptions," the things they would not move: The piano, the sofa, the king-size bed, the china cabinet, the steel filing cabinets, many "et ceteras." Not our agreement! We argued our case for two hours, while they loaded our lighter possessions. Art raged and retreated to another room to calm down.

"Do you think your husband will buy us lunch?" the head guy asked.

WHAT?

Nervously, I approached Art with this request. He stared, didn't say a word for a few minutes, then grabbed his keys and left to go get hamburgers. It's a surprising world we live in. This gesture precipitated another: During his absence, the movers confabbed and relented on their "embargo" stance and began to move everything.

By day's end, we sat on the floor of our new home sharing a tub of Kentucky Fried Chicken with our new best friends, celebrating our successful adventure in moving, thanks to the "King" and the "Colonel"!

Two hectic weeks later, we returned from the jungles of Venezuela to our "mansion" that had been on the market for FOUR years, confident that we had months to find and buy the perfect house. The dust had barely settled when the call came that we would once more have to move since this gigantic house had been sold.

"Not to fear," the realtor exclaimed, "there are many houses on the market and you can have your pick."

We decided we wanted the ugliest, oddest, most unsellable house she could find. It so happened there was one right across the street from us, she said, and we could bypass the middleman and walk our stuff over.

Of course, as always, there was one catch: The house was equipped with all built-in furniture, from the beds to the sofas. Great. We now possessed three living room suites and needed nary a one. The impetus to attempt this venture in the first place was to spare ourselves the time, trouble and money of putting our furniture in storage. Now, having MORE furniture than before, we were going to do exactly that!

Our new weird house came equipped with raccoons tapping on our plate glass window all night long, a hideous kitchen with RED and BLACK appliances, neatly tied used condoms in the plant shadowboxes, and all walls were mirrored (the owner was a bodybuilder). As icing on the cake, daylight spilled in from multiple holes throughout the house. Surely with this eclectic hovel, we would be graced with enough time to find our own home; it would be a cold day in hell before this unreasonable facsimile of a house sold.

Finally, we found a wonderful house for sale and our realtor called the next day to learn that it had sold the day before. The scenario was repeated two weeks later and we began to doubt the universe. But it does its own thing in mysterious ways.

Not long after our second disappointment, we got a call from Wichita that my father had fallen ill. I left immediately, not to return again for four months. My father died soon after I arrived in Wichita and Art and I decided to bring my paralyzed mother to Texas to live with us. If we had purchased the two homes we lost to others, they would not have worked for us. We now needed a very specific home for the three of us with bedrooms downstairs plus a separate living area for a live-in helper. Art had to find our ideal place on his own before I could return and resume our life. Oh, yeah, we also got the call that the "unsellable" house had sold. Has the world gone mad?

But life is good if you wait long enough. Art miraculously found the "perfect" house, flew to Kansas, loaded a U-Haul with my mother's possessions and drove the three of us "home."

The new house was, indeed, perfect. Mother's room was next to ours; the halls were wheelchair-accessible; there was a handicapped bathroom with walk-in shower; there was a sidewalk surrounding the house for a wheelchair stroll; and upstairs boasted a complete apartment for Dorothy, our wonderful new live-in caregiver. Unbelievable.

The old adage is true, anywhere you hang your hat is home. But the caveat is: Sometimes the perfect hat rack is hard to find.

****

"A NON-MERRY CHRISTMAS STORY!"

"Guess what my husband is giving me for Christmas," my friend said giddily, as she opened her front door to let me in.

"A hard time?" I quipped.

"No, silly. I found some beautiful diamond stud earrings in his jacket pocket along with a card, 'For My True Love!' I was going to take his jacket to the cleaners, but left it on the chair so I wouldn't ruin the surprise!"

I was thrilled for her. They had been going through a tough time, money-wise. She had given up her beloved art lessons and her bowling league to cut expenses. She also needed a new car since hers was 20 years old, but he had stressed to her that times were tough and they had to cut down on frivolous things. She agreed. To make ends meet, he started working many extra hours.

Christmas came and went and no diamond earrings. We never talked of it again. The next year was an especially bad one for them; first, her husband became ill, then bedridden, and then died in October. But she took care of him faithfully to his dying day and mourned his passing.

A week after his funeral, I went with her to his office to clean out his desk. His secretary greeted us at the entry to his office with swollen, red eyes. She had been crying. As she hugged my friend, she expressed her sympathy at his passing and said he would be greatly missed. As she put her cheek to my friend's lips, her hair was brushed back from her face. She was wearing the beautiful diamond stud earrings! And they were one inch from my friend's surprised eyes.

I was busy with a pressing job the following month, but in December we were able to plan for lunch and a movie and we met at her house. "Guess what my husband is giving me posthumously for Christmas," my friend said giddily, as she opened her front door to let me in.

"Diamond earrings!" I guessed wildly. Well, maybe not so "wildly," since large stones (bigger than the secretarial ones) already glistened from her earlobes. With her ringless fingers, she nonchalantly pushed her hair back behind her ears. She nodded and grinned.

"But that's not all. The package they came in was really special," she said, as she led me out to the garage. There sat a brand new red convertible with the top down. In the back seat of the car in a ratty cardboard box was the simple urn that contained her husband's ashes with its lid ajar.

"How about us going for a fun wind ride?" she enthusiastically invited!

****

EVERYTHING HAPPENS FOR A REASON, ONLY SOMETIMES YOU HAVE TO WAIT FOR YEARS TO FIND OUT WHAT THE HELL JUST HAPPENED!
-or-
MY DIVORCE, THE WORST AND BEST THING THAT EVER HAPPENED TO ME!

It was 1967 and I was riding high on life and blissfully naive to the world around me. My husband of two years, Dean Aiken, had gotten a job in Cape Canaveral, Florida and unceremoniously and abruptly uprooted me from my Kansas cocoon. Though I was 27 in people years, I still lacked worldly knowledge and the harsh reality it can sometimes deliver. Despite my dire predictions, I adjusted well to the move, we bought a fabulous new house, made exciting new friends, and I landed a job that I loved at Boeing. At my insistence and his reluctance, Dean and I applied for and had recently passed all the tests to appear on "Treasure Hunt," a TV game show filmed in Florida. The writers of the show had written our ad libs about the ocelot with whom we shared our home, and I was all prepared for bigger and better things after our appearance. All was well with the world, well, even better than "well."

One sunny day in June my husband arrived home from work and announced he had something to tell me. I imagined a trip to Europe, a large raise, or a piece of jewelry! He fixed me a drink and sat me down in the living room, pulled up another chair in front of me and delivered a death blow! He wanted a divorce.

After the dirty deed was final, my ex still kept in touch with me, picking the scab off the wound each time. He had paid some of his lawyer's legal fees with his very expensive golf clubs and since I was a good friend of the lawyer's wife, my ex would call me when he wanted to play golf and I would dutifully retrieve his clubs from my friend for a round or two.

Wanting to find myself and where I belonged, I drifted around - literally - which included working as a hostess on a cruise ship and then moving to Fort Lauderdale where I worked for Kelley Girls until settling on a secretarial position. My ex kept in touch with me regularly, even during his three subsequent marriages. He would give my name and phone number as a referral to his devastated wives and advise them to call me and find out how I handled the divorce so well. High praise indeed from such a scoundrel. I spoke to the crying wives about him only in expletives, told them it was the best thing that could happen to them. I hope I helped them somewhat.

But finally, at 33 years of age, I decided on what I wanted to be when I grew up. When I was young I had high aspirations and wanted to be an elevator operator (Watch your step, please), but now I wanted to be a court reporter. So I enrolled in night school and began my journey. I checked the "Help Wanted" ads regularly, though, since I was unhappy in my current position. One weekend, there was a large ad in the newspaper. A court reporting firm was looking for typists. I felt this was a match made in heaven, so I applied on my lunch hour the next day. A young Latino guy who managed the firm interviewed me and, after his first choice didn't work out, a week later gave me the nod and I began work shortly thereafter.

In my second week, the owner of the firm made his appearance, and I felt it was kismet. Everything happens for a reason, you know. I had been dating older men and he was. He oozed Southern charm and called me "Darlin'" and I was smitten. He asked me out for a drink that night, dragging the manager along, combining business with pleasure, and I knew this was the beginning of something big. Everything was going great, until he received a phone call during our office/bar ménage à trois and had to hurry off, ostensibly on business.

In the intervening years since that night in 1974, my ex-husband went through three other wives. Then, following a stroke, he suffered with severe disabilities for three years before dying. God rest his wicked soul. I, on the other hand, found my soul mate that night in the bar. The young Latino manager turned out to be Arturo Zapata, my second and last husband. On our first date, it was love at dawn's light and we have been together ever since; he's never left nor have I.

So, the worst thing to happen to me turned out to be the best thing to happen to me, ever!

Cliché though it may be, everything really does happen for a reason. But sometimes you have to wait a few years for the saying to work its wonders and you figure it out!

****

TO HELL WITH TRADITION!

Neither of us remembers who asked whom to get married (apparently nobody wants to take the blame for it), but for some reason we decided to get married on June 17, 1978 (though we count our first date in February, 1974, as our anniversary).

We didn't want to make a big deal out of our wedding since we had been living together for so long, but I at least wanted to do more than a trip to Las Vegas' Love Chapel.

I looked long and hard for an appropriate outfit to be married in, but nothing seemed to fit (in more ways than one). On a trip to Wichita, Kansas to visit my parents, I complained about my lack of finding a dress. My father stepped up to the plate and said, "Let's go shopping" (words I had never heard him utter before in that order), and when he added, "and I'll buy you a dress," I had to check the address of the house to make sure I was in the right place.

I didn't imagine I would find my dress in Wichita, but in our first store, whether by luck or by force, only a block away from the home I grew up in, I found exactly what I had been looking for. It was a long, flowing red strapless gown with a gossamer cape-type overcoat and a large, billowy red flower in the middle of my breasts. PERFECT. I was a "Scarlet Woman" and this set the tone for the rest of the wedding decorations.

My father was pleased with his purchase and said it was lots cheaper than the first time I got married, and then proceeded to bring out all the receipts from my first wedding that he had been keeping for me. Did I want them? Yes, it would make really good starter for our fire next winter.

From there, the rest was easy. We had invitations printed with red geraniums (it was now "our" flower) running down the side, and chose a George Bernard Shaw quote as our mantra: "Everything happens to everybody sooner or later, if there is time enough."

There was no problem renting the venue since our house in South Bend, Indiana shared its lawn with a public park situated across the street from the St. Joseph River whose trees and rippling music only added to the ambiance of the surroundings. We would enjoy the reception on our second-floor, enclosed patio that could hold and comfortably seat 50, plus it overlooked the park with the Indiana sunset as backdrop. I rented folding chairs to nestle among the trees, bought huge, four-foot high geraniums, also some smaller potted ones to put on the trees along with candelabras from a garage sale. Art's boss, a federal judge, agreed to officiate the ceremony and asked if he couldn't wear his judge's gown. Of course, that made the setting more iconic and ironic. I painted white tablecloths with acrylic red geraniums. My aunt had given me my grandmother's wedding ring years earlier, so that would be great as a stunt-double, stand-in ring since we were planning on honeymooning in Colombia and buying matching emerald wedding rings. Art got into the swing of things and bought me an emerald pendant for "something new" (I vowed never to take it off) and himself a red tie. (Wow! Control thyself!)

Everything fell into place and we were good to go. But then Murphy got involved. Art forgot to mail his family the invitations, so they arrived for a visit, only to be told there was a wedding the next day and nobody brought any dress-up clothes. So we fought. I wanted the mariachis that I had arranged for but Art said they cost too much and didn't want to drive to Chicago to pick them up. So we fought. Our Red Velvet cake was not ready to be picked up as scheduled. So we fought. I wore my emerald necklace to play tennis and lost it and we spent hours searching the courts with no luck. So we fought.

The big day arrived. "I do," the first words we had exchanged in 24 hours, echoed in the park and I looked down at my grandmother's ring on my finger. Then we looked at each other and forgot everything else. It was a wonderful wedding. Our party adjourned to the patio with everyone collecting and carrying their own seats to the party.

The photographer wanted to snap our photo cutting the cake, so I rushed inside the house to find a knife. But the only cake knife I found was one engraved, "Marilyn and Dean, 1965," and I feared that would not bode well for this marriage, so opted for a huge butcher knife instead.

I hurried back outside, assumed my position next to the groom and held the knife over the cake. Art lovingly covered my hand with his and pushed down hard while the photographer snapped for posterity our great accomplishment ... but wait, there's shooting blood. I had the knife upside down and had cut an artery! Mayhem!

I would not leave the party to go to the hospital. This was my wedding day. I steadfastly refused and Art gave up and found a huge red bath towel (how considerate, to make sure he used the right theme color, though later he admitted he just grabbed one haphazardly; there goes romance!) and wrapped it around my finger and duct-taped it. Viola! I was fine, though I have to admit the margaritas helped ease the pain.

Months later I went back to Wichita with photos (omitting the one of my screaming, terrified face as we cut the cake). I took them with me to visit my aunt and proudly showed her the ring on my finger, knowing she would be aglow with the knowledge I wore her mother's ring. She looked down at it and then at me. "Why, Honey, that's not your grandmother's ring. That's just the one she found at the laundry where she worked."

To make sure we weren't snake-bit by our wedding, on our honeymoon in the Amazon, we started a new tradition. We bought everything in twos – one for me and one for him – just in case the statistics kicked in and a pending divorce reared its ugly head. But I'm happy to say, with double décor, we now have the most crowded house in the neighborhood!

****

THINGS I LEARNED AT MY MOTHER'S KNEE
(AND OTHER BODY PARTS)

My mother, Dolly Jackson Bellinghausen, instructed me in the traditional rules of religion, etiquette, and fair play (pray daily, always place the salad fork on the left, don't cancel a date on anyone if you get a better offer, etc.). But it was her unconventional teachings that proved most valuable in shaping my character.

HOW TO GIVE AND ACCEPT ANY GIFT: For the 50 Christmases that she shared her life with me, she unashamedly gave a dollar to one and all, no matter their status in her life (albeit a silver dollar with the current year on it, still a dollar). My poor father sometimes went from bank to bank on Christmas Eve trying to find coins to meet her satisfaction, but not without grumbling. At our family Christmas exchanges she was given in turn "used flash cubes", toilet paper cardboard rolls, used stamps. The recipients of her coins always acted surprised and happy with their present. Likewise, my mother always acted as if a collection of used toilet paper cardboard rolls was exactly what she had been wishing for, and made it a point to later show the gift-giver what she had done with them (she was a crafter). To this day, instead of store-bought gifts, I give friends and family the fruits of my meager talent, such as handmade cards (recycled paper), painted books (Salvation Army finds where I embellish the pages), and leather toy camels (regally decorated with garage sale trinkets). Although sometimes, at the annual Christmas party I host, it's a class of something I've learned, like how to cut a bonsai tree, decorate a gingerbread house, make sushi, or to arrange mosaic pieces on wooden crosses (bought on sale at Michael's after Easter).

HOW TO FOLLOW YOUR DREAM: As a poor little girl in the early 1900s, Mother dreamed of playing the piano. Each day she would draw a keyboard into the dirt and each day her older brothers would run through it recklessly or kick it silly. So she grew prolific at painting keyboards and practiced diligently on her newly-keyed dirt piano. She taught herself the notes from used sheet music given to her by her mother's friend. She bought her first and only piano by paying $1 a week out of her meager salary. I have that piano now and though she paid for weekly lessons for me for ten years and told me I would be the life of every party, that dream of hers, not mine, never came to fruition. She tried to instill the love of piano in me; it didn't take. But I do treasure her piano and use it as an easel on which to stand framed photographs and those leather camels, but her lesson of perseverance in your chosen avocation has not been lost on me.

HOW TO STAY HAPPY: My mother was one of nine children in a family that had little. She made her own toys: Paper dolls cut from Sears catalogues, small villages made from the cardboard of cereal boxes, etc. As she grew older, she still retained her youthful love of creating and being involved with children. She was my Girl Scout leader, she was my dancing teacher's aide, she was my twirling troupe's chaperone on our field trips; she was always there. I learned that you have to let a person find their own way. My loves are tennis, mah jongg, writing and art, nothing like hers, but the path to happiness is the same. Embrace your joys.

HOW TO SAVE MONEY: Though my father's salary increased over the years to a goodly sum, they continued to live in the same little shoebox of a home and didn't care if they entertained their rich friends in humble surroundings. My mother would buy one chocolate turtle to divide into thirds for "The Three B's" (her nickname for the three of us – my father, my mother and me) for dessert. If our paper napkins were still clean after the end of a meal, she would write our names on them for the next day. She would limit me to a half inch of scotch tape per envelope. Today I make sure my paper napkins are unusable at the end of every meal so I can throw them away. I buy chocolate turtles and eat the whole box in one setting. My budget for scotch tape sometimes makes me blush in embarrassment because I use it with such exuberant abandon when wrapping presents or mailing packages. My savings are small but my life is filled with many small pleasures.

HOW TO TREASURE YOUR FRIENDS: My mother loved to play bridge and was a master player. Yet she enjoyed a bridge game every Friday night with her best friend and neighbor who couldn't seem to get the hang of the game and would trump her ace on a regular basis. An avid player myself, I was incredulous at her patience and asked her how she could continue to play with such a horrendous player week after week, and she said, "She is my friend." And that explained it all.

HOW TO REMEMBER THE GOOD TIMES AND FORGET THE BAD: My mother was a scrap-booker before "scrap-booking" was popular. She collected all sorts of memorabilia to help remember the good times (ticket stubs, napkins, cards from friends and, inexplicably, daily she'd cut the date from the newspaper so she could add a highlight of that day). My father was a relentless driver, so we took many road trips. As we sped each year from Kansas to Colorado to Canada to California to Mexico and back to Kansas in two weeks, my mother would sleep in the front seat and wake only when the car stopped. Wherever we were, she would ask to be taken to a Woolworth's, buy a postcard of whatever we saw there, and then spend the night writing and pasting in her scrapbook. The next day would bring the same schedule: Sleep, stop, buy, write, paste. I now follow her lead but with a twist that doesn't take up so much time or room. I take photos daily; with the new technology, I can capture hundreds of thousands of all the positive and colorful things in my life to look at whenever I forget how good things really are. It's also great for those of us inclined to have short memory retention without reams of scrapbooks to store.

HOW PAINT IS YOUR FRIEND. Mother painted everything (our turtle, garage sale treasures, cans, wood and plastic). With my mother as a living example, I realized the immense importance of a happy, colorful life and I took this precious morsel of advice to heart. I now paint almost daily. Aside from many canvasses and sketch books, I've dyed not only my hair but also the hair of my white cats with cake coloring. Also I've painted books, furniture, a coffin, skulls (moose, javelina, deer and goat), a colonoscopy photo, kitchen tiles, food (particularly pastas, potatoes and rice), my old bike from 1950, my laundry refrigerator (the history of the Aztecs) and anything that looks dull. I never leave home without my American Express card and my paint collection. On vacation, I've painted the walking sticks my husband cuts for me, rocks to look like the painted houses of Newfoundland, leaves, feathers and bones from 4,000 year old creatures that now decorate a cave in Spain where we lived for a month. On the Amazon River, I finished painting the jungle mural on our hotel room's walls. Thanks to my mother, paint is not only my friend but is, as the Japanese say, my "nakama" (better than best friend).

Other Aesopian morals she imparted to me that weren't as useful were:

ALWAYS CARRY A DIME FOR A PHONE CALL IN A HANKIE. (Does anyone still use hankies and where can you find a pay phone if you're not in London and they wouldn't take dimes anyway?)

ALWAYS MAKE YOUR HUSBAND A MEAL FOR DINNER EVEN IF YOU ARE MAD AT HIM. (This one was hard to follow but I have, though with an added twist: Either burn the food, don't salt it, use food coloring to "enhance it" or do something that proves you are no pushover and it's not over until he apologizes.)

NEVER STICK YOUR HAND IN A DIRT HOLE AT THE INSISTENCE OF YOUR BROTHERS. (This one never applied to me but apparently she fell victim to her siblings' suggestions multiple times and always discovered worms.)

ALWAYS WASH YOUR BOBBIE PINS AFTER EACH USE. I was such a rebel in my youth that I used them several times in a row before washing them and leaving them to dry and develop a rust coating and had to buy new ones before their time.

ALWAYS IRON YOUR SHEETS AND UNDERWEAR. I just pretended like I never heard this one.

But my favorite "words of wisdom" uttered by my mother were:

NEVER FORGET YOUR ROOTS. She may have been talking about dying your hair before the roots show and your friends talk about you, but I took this one to mean to never forget her. As if I ever could!

****

THE SORORITY YEARS!

In 1964, when I was 18, some thoroughly modern women came to my Wichita high school and said they were recruiting young ladies for a worldwide social sorority intended specifically for young ladies, enabling them to get together, talk about recent things, do some good work and meet new friends. It seemed right up my alley since at the time there were few organized activities for girls at our school and elsewhere. I was just starting to hear about "women's lib" and I wanted to get on the bandwagon. I joined immediately and never missed a meeting.

The sorority stood me in good stead when I moved from Wichita to Cocoa Beach to Fort Lauderdale to South Bend. At each place I had a new set of already built-in friends awaiting me but after our final move to Texas, I had been overloaded with new friends, felt completely liberated, had recently discovered a new sport, tennis, and I never got around to reupping; the bandwagon had served its purpose, and this chapter in my book of life seemed closed forever.

1964. Fast forward 50 years later to 2015. My phone rang in Pearland, Texas. It was a Country Place neighbor introducing herself and saying she belonged to a chapter of my old sorority, and had heard I had recently moved to the neighborhood, someone had told her I spoke at the Women's Discussion Group here, and she wanted to invite me to a meeting.

Wow, I thought, they're good at locating wayward women. My social calendar since arriving had been filled to the brim with activities and I knew I couldn't handle another group/club, but I wanted to see how times had changed with this '50s group, so I agreed to attend their meeting. But I promised myself and Art ... who remembered helping me with all the activities of this group in our early years and who said he didn't want to join again, so count him out ... that I would not be adding another function to my repertoire. No matter how much they begged me to rejoin this group, I just had to draw the line somewhere. I hoped they didn't hold it against me if I refused, but I steeled myself to be adamant in my denial of another term.

The day of, I had garage saleing in the morning, but on my way out, I listened to a recording of a telephone message the day earlier, and my sorority sister/neighbor asked if I wouldn't bring a resume and a synopsis of my life so she could incorporate it into the record. I knew I wouldn't have time to prepare anything on my return since there were many treasures waiting to be found and the sales would be plentiful because it was the first warm day in February, so I figured they would just have to do without, I wasn't going to belong to their group anyway, so it didn't matter.

I arrived at the appointed hour exactly on time and ... like the over-70 crowd at Country Place ... everyone was already there (it seems the unspoken rule is: For every year over 70 you are, you arrive five minutes early to any gathering. 71, five minutes; 72, ten minutes, you get the picture). There was a group of about a dozen women gathered in the hostess' living room sitting in a circle around a coffee table like a Norman Rockwell painting on a 1950 Saturday Evening Post cover. When I walked into the room, my mentor shh'ed them and they quieted down obediently and all turned in my direction. She said, "Ladies, I want to introduce you to Marilyn Zapata, our guest speaker today." WHAT!!!!!!!????????

I turned to her, mouth agape, and gave the universal signal of hands up and shoulders shrugged as in "What the hell?" And she said, "Oh, didn't you know you were the guest speaker?"

I fumbled around thinking of a great comeback and finally, cleverly came up with, "No!"

"I thought I told you. I guess not. I'm sorry."

"Oh," I said, "I imagine I can come up with something." So, off I went and chattered about my books, my art, multiple et ceteras, and rambled on for 20 minutes, until, at a pause while I was taking a breath, the hostess cleared her throat.

"What a delightful presentation. Thanks, Marilyn."

A small round of applause.

"Now we can adjourn to the dining room for lunch."

A large round of applause.

And that was it. After lunch, I hung around for a few minutes and said "Goodbye" to everyone and told them how much I enjoyed their company and how I didn't realize how much I missed belonging to the sorority. I was mainly waiting to decline the invitation to join their group but it was never forthcoming. Hmm.

Every day since, I've thought about calling my neighbor and saying how much I'd like to join the sorority again. I'm going to wait a few weeks before I do, though, and make them suffer a little while longer.

****

After I wrote this story, I sent it to Ginny, my friend in Fort Lauderdale, Florida 45 years ago, who had been in this sorority with me. She wrote back a memory that made me giggle big time.

She said that I had begged her to join this national society since I insisted I needed her there to liven things up. She finally consented when I threw in a free meal at Bachelors III (Joe Namath's restaurant) and only then did she learn of the rigorous initiation rituals and the many things she had to learn before she could call herself a "sister." She had second and third thoughts about it, but decided we might have fun together. I helped her learn the rules, ropes and regulations and vigilantly repeated with her the ritual "pledges" that we recited at the beginning and end of each meet until she had them memorized "pitch perfect". Eventually the time came when she was ready for her "baptism". At the next meeting, all members were present and taking the process of her induction into our group very seriously. The room grew silent, members gathered into a circle and joined hands, the lights went dim, the candles were lit, and the president of our group spoke welcoming words to Ginny, then asked the group who would sponsor her into our glorious sisterhood. All eyes turned toward me. I said, "Not me. I never saw her before in my life!"

****

MENSA SHMENSA!!

When my future husband, Art Zapata, interviewed me for a job as a transcriber in his court reporting office, I just knew we had a future together. I thought along the lines of working together for a few years and then moving on to my own reporting firm, not doing absolutely everything together for the next 40 years and counting, as it turned out.

It was 1974, and at that point in my life I was trying to change myself, inside and out. With the help of Cosmopolitan, the social front was looking better. Also I was in the second semester of court reporting school and was attempting to distance myself from the engineering firm where I had worked as a secretary for two years, since everyone there was embroiled in various levels of chicanery, theft and debauchery (but that's another story altogether and the statute of limitations hasn't run out yet).

I read the Want Ads every day hoping to find the perfect job to accelerate myself down my chosen path which consisted of morphing into a court reporter like the one I had seen on Perry Mason. I was impressed with her calm demeanor and erect posture as she sat at her little machine and cooly gazed at the world all the while recording every word being said by Perry and his cronies. She dressed beautifully and garnered respect from everyone in the courtroom. (Years earlier I had used this same silly Batman logic to delude myself into thinking I wanted to be a cruise director and failed miserably at it once given the chance, but the day still lives in infamy in my mind. So, the old adage is true, some people never learn.)

On a cool fall day in 1974, I happened upon a call of destiny in the form of an ad written by Art Zapata: "Transcriber Wanted. Busy Court Reporting Firm. Must have above-average typing skills." A match made in heaven, and I wasn't talking about the boss.

During our interview Mr. Zapata grilled me on my abilities.

"How fast can you type?"

"Oh, I can easily type 100 words a minute."

"Oh, really? How about your shorthand skills?"

"120 on a slow day," I bragged.

"What other qualifications do you have?

"I'm a MENSA!" (I had taken the IQ test for this genius organization three years earlier and had scored beyond my expectations and, in spite of having ingested two beers during the test, landed in the upper one-half of one percent in intelligence in the world. I am quite proud of this accomplishment and somehow I usually manage to work that fact into every conversation I have.)

"And you're proud of that?" He said incredulously.

(He seems to be snickering! How odd? I wonder what he meant by that.) "Yes, I'm very proud of that" I hopefully said indignantly.

"Oh, all right." Slight laugh. "Well, Marilyn, I've already hired someone for this position. I will keep your resume on file though and call you if things don't work out with her."

(WHAT? Is he out of his mind? Doesn't he know he's missing out on a great thing? I think I'm going to cry, I want the job so badly.) All of that went through my mind in a flash, but what I said was, "Thanks, Mr. Zapata." And I held my head high and walked out the door. But cried myself to sleep that night.

Fast forward two weeks and my phone rings.

"This is Art Zapata. Are you still interested in the job, Marilyn?"

"Yes, I am. I can start tomorrow." (But what I meant was: Hell, yes. And I'm also signing up for 40 years of happiness, taking the road less traveled and savoring the idiosyncrasies of life. I knew I was making the best decision of my life.)

It wasn't until two weeks later, after our first date (he never went home or left my side from that date forward) that Art explained his reaction to my "admission" that I was a MENSA.

It seems that in Spanish, his first language, "mensa" means a foolish, stupid woman!!

****

98

THANKS, I GUESS!

At one of our Red Hat meetings, a friend, Julia Schwartz, came up to me afterwards and said, "You know, I just love your 'Senior Moments' book. Are you going to be writing another one?" (Little did she or I realize she was going to be included in this one.)

(Wow, I thought. I think I've found my fan base and a market for these stories.)

"I'm going to publish another book along the same lines due out next year titled, 'A Funny Thing Happened on My Way to the Crypt,'" I said, "and I'll be sure to let you know when it's available."

She acted excited at the prospect and explained: "You know, I don't sleep very well, but whenever I can't, I grab your book that I keep next to my bed and after a story or two, I find myself nodding off. And I just wanted to thank you for that."

After much deliberation, I've decided to take her words as a great compliment, though I might be grading that one on a curve.

****

GARAGE SALEING STORIES
or
HOW TO FIND THINGS THAT YOU DIDN'T EVEN KNOW YOU WANTED!

In my previous book, I had a chapter on a few garage saleing experiences, but thereafter I've had so many more that I just have to share them here and get them immortalized on paper before they get tossed and I make room in my memory for other things.

THE RETURN OF THE TRAY!

One cold Saturday morning in February during the second winter of the year, a trio of intrepid thrifters (Susan Columbus, Chica Lopez and myself) couldn't find enough garage sales in Pearland so I headed the van down 518 almost all the way to Friendswood where I used to live.

We found a few more sales but nothing of import and, spotting one more sign before we hit the city limits, we woefully decided this would be our last stop-and-shop of the day. Good signage led us to a big home with a circular drive and big gates in front, one emblazoned with a large banner that read, "Jesus Loves You." Oh, Lord, I thought, there goes any chance of haggling!

There was a multitude of tables filling the driveway, each loaded with "stuff," so we excitedly hurried through the pearly gates. The first interesting thing I picked up looked oddly familiar and I examined it momentarily before exclaiming, "Hey, I made this!" It was a mosaicked wooden tray I had created with due diligence and bleeding hands (thanks to all the sharp shards) and had really hated to part with it but part with it I did due to our downsizing two years earlier. I turned to the woman standing guard of her wares and asked, "Did you, by any chance, get this at a garage sale?"

Then a booming voice behind me: "Of course. You made it. You made half of the things I have in my home here!" I turned around and there stood Jose, the best customer of my "Mother of All Garage Sales," when we moved from Friendswood and I was forced to part with too many treasures to remember due to a 1,000-square-foot loss of living space. I watched as the large, burly, lovable guy came up and hugged me. Then I remembered the details that the devil is in, and hugged him back.

That memorable day of yore (I had six helpers, stuff all over the house full to capacity, nothing labeled, cars parked blocks away filling the neighborhood, and hundreds of customers streaming into my home), Jose had arrived early and stayed all day, taking only a lunch break and subsequently returning with his wife who, following the lead of her husband, was also a good shopper. He imbibed many of the margaritas I offered my favorite customers and kept bundling up his purchases and taking them to his vehicle parked permanently out front (we should have charged for parking) and then returning for more. At the end of the day, as we wearily closed the garage door, we realized he was still with us and reluctant to leave, until Art offered him an armful of "freebies" and gently guided him to his "Grapes of Wrath" loaded truck.

Later, upon tallying my profits from the day, I realized Jose had spent $250 on my good and bad "stuff." And now here I was at his garage sale where half of his tables were laden with my old, "bad stuff" but also some of my hand-made "good stuff."

"I thought you moved to Mexico," (sometimes I tell strangers too many things).

"No, we are settled in Pearland as we speak. But where is my margarita?"

He explained that after that glorious day of buying and drinking, he had given up liquor and was now a tea-totaler; and apparently a smoke-free one at that, as I noted his used "hookah" on the table.

Looking around the grounds, I vowed to be on a mission to rescue and recycle some of my art that I had unwillingly had to part with. So, I went in search of some "good" piece that had been formerly mine. I found a birch bark strip painting I made for Art of a loon when we went to Wisconsin, but Jose wanted $45 for it and was adamant about the price (as well he should be of an original Zapata). There was a large box of broken talavera dishes I had prepared for a big wall mural ... also too high priced for me at $100. "How about this altered book?" "$50." Darn, he was really good at this! But I hated that I couldn't afford any of my own artwork!

I wouldn't give up, though, since I knew I definitely had to get something of mine from this garage sale, if only to watch Art's face when I told him about my reclamation project. So, I returned to my mosaic tray that had started the whole memory lane thing; it had a measly $15 tag on it. Raising my eyebrows, "Would you take $1 for this, please?" I sang. I think the "please" did it. He paused, contemplated the offer, then smiled, scooped up the tray, handed it to me, hugged me and said, "It's yours," words that were music to my ears. What a coup!

Moral of the Story: Some things are destined to be yours for keeps but sometimes you have to wait a few years for their return if you ever let them out of your sight. This applies to "things", "people," and "memories"!

****

SOME PEOPLE NEVER LEARN!

Bobbie and I were on our way to another garage sale early one crisp fall morning when I got pulled over by a policeman younger than I can ever remember being. He was kind enough but didn't want to even listen the alibi about waking up at 6:30 so we could beat the crowd to the sales. I took it like a wo-man and didn't balk since I knew I was in the wrong though it felt right at the time.

It had been a while since I had gotten a ticket (also with Bobbie going through a neighborhood looking for garage sales - I think I see a pattern here), but the last time my defensive driving class at the comedy club had been so entertaining that I was even looking forward to taking the class again. So, I signed up for another Saturday all-dayer in League City.

Like a bad habit, I woke up early the scheduled Saturday morning, thinking I was going garage saleing. When I discovered that I was too early for my class that started at 9:00, I decided to go ahead and enjoy a garage sale or two before heading to the class. My first stop was in the neighborhood next to ours. I followed the signs and took a left turn, only to discover I had turned right in front of a police car parked at the STOP sign. There was one on my side also but I had been too busy following other signs to take this one in and obey. As I passed him, he held up his hand like he was saying "Hi" in Cherokee so I cheeringly waved at him too. But I immediately re-evaluated the gesture five feet down the street and definitely it was an "H" word, but instead of "Hi", he was saying, "Halt."

I sped up then since I knew he would have to turn around to catch me and that it would take some time to give chase. I turned left, then right, then right again, then left, then panting and sweating pulled into a driveway and threw myself prone in the front seat. As I lay there, all I could think of was: What am I going to do when he taps on the window with his gun? At 73 years of age, was he going to put me in jail or just laugh?

I gave him a good half hour, before I rose up out of my hiding place, looked around, and took off again, taking a back road out of the neighborhood. I circled around my own neighborhood so I wouldn't have to use the main highway and accidentally (pun intended) run into him again.

Once safely at the defensive driving class, the first question by the moderator was: "When was your last run-in with the law?" I held up my hand and said, "Sixty minutes ago." We all laughed, but I didn't mean it. I was still shaking over my hour-ago run-in and found nothing funny about it, only thankfulness that I didn't have to explain to my husband about getting a ticket garage saleing on my way to defensive driving for another ticket garage saleing.

After the defensive driving class was finally over (and the policeman's shift was too, I hoped), just to make sure I had truly made a clean getaway, I went 20 miles out of my way to get home after class. I had lived to garage sale another day. And another. And another.

****

SCORING BIG!

Through the years and walking up to thousands of garage sales, it stands to reason and the odds are in my favor that we will find some fabulous things. Now, I've never come across a "Picasso" or a mint gold coin, but I have found some pretty amazing treasures.

MARILYN AND THE PHILOSOPHERS!

Going garage saleing alone is something I am not prone to do, but sometimes the "call of the wild chase" is just too great to ignore. Driving home from tennis one day, I spotted an "Estate Sale" sign that was handwritten, a dead give-away that it really isn't an estate sale handled by pros where they charge extra for holding the sale, and overprice everything. To make sure the customers will pay too much, they display it better (but I love to rummage through piles), clean up the merchandise to make it presentable (but I prefer a tarnished silver tray, it will be cheaper), the price tags are printed (but we prefer the oral transaction where the prices are arbitrarily made up on the spot and differ from customer to customer, since that is when you can really barter). Besides the handwritten sign, another amateur clue was that it was written on the side of a cardboard box and mounted on a metal stand formerly used for a political campaign sign (another omen of good prices since they would not have experience in holding garage sales and would not be aware of the caliber of clientele this type of sign draws in).

I made a sharp U-turn into a small cottage's driveway with a fastidious yard and picket fence that promised well-kept goods inside. Upon entering the home, I was met by a kind, elderly lady who introduced herself as "Hazel," who apparently was the owner of the home and its contents. She seemed lonely and I sensed she wanted to talk (this was late in the afternoon, another good time for a bargain).

I learned from Hazel that her younger sister, a former "sister" (nun), had lived in this home but recently moved cross country to marry her childhood beau who had lost his wife of 50 years. She had told Hazel that she could have the house and everything in it to do with as she wished. Hazel and I were very happy for her and I loved that story and knew I was definitely going to buy something this day, whether I wanted it or not.

I scoured the kitchen chock full of dainty teacups and saucers, milk glass and jelly glasses. Nothing for me.

The bedroom held clothes too prim and proper and too drab to catch my attention, not to mention they were all one-numeral sizes. Nothing for me.

The bathroom contained dainty finger towels (never used, they never are), perfumes of various sized vials and shapes (I've been warned by Art never to buy anything with the word "eau" in it again from garage sales). Nothing for me.

But the living room had a glass case which caught my eye. Inside I found several crosses I just had to have (at the time I had 500 on my bedroom wall - and by "my bedroom wall," I mean that Art wouldn't let me spread the wealth and said if I wanted that many crosses on the wall, I could put them all on my side of the room). But there was one particular cross that really drew me to it. I spent eight years in a Catholic school with Dominican nuns as teachers, and had stared many hundreds of times into that distinguishable cross that hung around my teachers' necks as they leaned over my desk to check my homework. A very common cross it was, but it had a screw in the bottom of it and I knew what that meant: Inside there was a distant martyr's relic that surely had been sealed and ceremoniously blessed by a pope. The cross was marked $20 and I knew its future lie in being the centerpiece of my collection. But first there was bargaining to be done.

I took it to the front where Hazel stood guard over her cigar box of dollar bills and showed her what I was interested in. It's not hard for me to plead ignorance since it comes naturally but I asked her innocently if that was her best price. She was nodding her head already and had opened her mouth to speak, affirmatively I was sure, when a large man with huge hands reached over my shoulder trying to grab my cross saying to Hazel, "Well, if she doesn't want it for twenty, I sure do." Even with a cross in my hand, I thought bad thoughts toward that man, smattered with lots of bleeped words. Of course, haggling was now out of the question.

But it was mine and Hazel said she was glad I picked it. I had another bad thought, had she planted that man and used him when I tried to outsmart her? Naw, couldn't be; I'm smarter than that.

As she wrapped up my treasure, she explained that since her sister had been a religious in a former life, she figured that's where it came from, but she had no other idea of its origin or anything. She said she had opened it and found another little cross inside, so that's the reason it was more expensive. I said I agreed and couldn't wait to get home to see for myself.

As I left, I turned around for another look through the living room and I saw Hazel and Mr. Interruptus giggling with each other. Oh, my, I was sure I had been taken. Not a first, but a disappointment nonetheless. Still, the cross was a nice one and interesting, I rationalized.

When I arrived home, first things first. I laid the cross out on a white towel and opened the rusty screw. Inside was, indeed, another little cross sealed on its back with red wax. Then I turned it over. There were tiny slivers of bone on discolored discs the size of a baby's toenail, next to small yellowed-paper banners that bore the names of "S. Thom. Aq. C." and "S. Cath. Sen." and three others. Maybe this was real after all. I couldn't wait to research my find, but in the meantime I just nailed it on my cross wall and woke up each morning gazing at that wall in awe.

Fast forward at least 20 years, and as I sat at my computer writing this story, I switched over to Google to search for the cryptic names I had found inside the cross. I was definitely not taken. As it turns out, I was the takee. How lucky I was in finding this religious treasure. How could I have doubted sweet Hazel, thinking she had perpetrated a hoax?

It turns out I acquired, at a garage sale, for a mere $20, minuscule relics of Saint Thomas Aquinas, a philosopher/theologian, who died in 1274 and Saint Catherine of Siena, also a scholastic philosopher/theologian, who died in 1380. They must be turning over in their respective tombs as I tell this story. Belated thanks to Hazel, Tom and Cate for such a gift!

****

THE WHOOPING COFFIN!

In April, 1999, I received an excited telephone call from my sister-in-law, Chica. She had been watching the Deborah Duncan Show, a local Houston talk show in front of a live audience, and they issued a call-out for anyone who had found some "exceptional treasures" at garage sales. They wanted to devote a whole segment to appraisals of said bargains. I couldn't dial the number fast enough.

Three years earlier I had stumbled upon one of my eeriest and best conversation pieces for the living room: A coffin, painted bright red, sold by a man who said he had gotten it for his wife for her 40th birthday (must be love) and had filled it with presents, then nailed it shut. Now they had no use for it. (Really?) He wanted an outstanding $5 for it but on Gestapo-like interrogation and incessant whining while negotiating, we managed to arrive at a better price of $3. I was ecstatic. Art not so much when I drug it into the house and showed it to him. His reaction was reminiscent of mine when my cat once drug a mouse into the house and triumphantly presented it to me. I failed to appreciate its value, as did Art my new coffin.

In the intervening years I covered the wooden sarcophagus with turquoise blue paint and on the lid I painted a large Virgin of Guadalupe surrounded by angels, hovering above a Mexican village and desert scene with cacti; on the sides, more angels and stars. I loved it! On the Inside Art lovingly ... and against his better judgment ... made me shelves where I kept my collection of Virgins of Guadalupe that I would add to each time we'd visit Mexico.

I knew Deborah would love this find, and I was asked to be on the show the minute I said, "coffin." Her coordinator said to bring friends so I rounded up Chica (her find was a 50-cent milk glass latticed bowl), Bobbie (her find was a $1 antique doll), Maureen Viaclovsky (her find was a 25-cent carnival glass candy dish) and Naomi Lopez, Chica's daughter, who wanted to go along with us but refused to acknowledge she even slightly knew us and each time the camera caught her, she was laughing. I also carried a cow's hide that I had roped for only $20.

Deborah didn't have many respondents, so she had to change her format to include not only garage sale items but others as well, and to have them appraised by a man from The Antiques Roadshow.

We were greeted warmly into the studio and I was informed that they would be filming a "teaser" about me with my coffin; and to shock the audience, they draped the cow skin over the coffin and wanted me to make the "big reveal"! I was ready for my closeup, Mr. DeMille, and also my 15 minutes of fame, Andy!"

SHOW TIME! The antiques estimator pooh-poohed Bobbie's doll as not even qualified to be on the show, told Maureen she had barely broken even on her carnival glass and informed Chica she had made the best find and could probably resell her milk glass bowl for $3. What a downer for us all!

But then I unveiled my coffin to a gasp from the audience and I beamed! Then the guy said my precious treasure was probably worth nothing except to me for sentimental value! WHAT? I told him it had no sentimental value, but it was brand new and had never been used and must be worth something, plus I spent hours of my "precious" time painting it. It was like pleading your case to the homeowner's tax department, he was steadfast in his valuation and wouldn't budge from his opinion! Deborah took my side and said it was fabulous and unique, and then the curtain came down on our parade. Face time on TV: Three minutes. I felt I was still owed another 12 minutes to fill out my 15 minutes, but there was nothing I could do about it.

We all were a little offput by the sound rejection of our "treasures" as being worth nothing, but even that could not bring down our fun day on television. Our appearances really began to pay off the next weekend when we went garage saleing again. That Saturday I was recognized four times, "Say, weren't you on the Deborah Duncan Show last week?" Once when I had just gotten out of the car at the end of the seller's driveway, a woman yelled, "Here comes "Famous"!" The next week, it dropped to only two recognitions, but for months thereafter, at least once an outing I'd hear, "Here comes the coffin lady!" or "Look, we've got royalty at our sale," or "What's Deborah Duncan really like?"

At six months out, my run of fame seemed to be over. Then several years later, the show went into reruns, and it was déjà vu all over again. My minutes of fame left now came to 11 more promised minutes.

And it continues. Fast forward more than a decade. In 2015, I wrote "Great Day Houston," a local live show hosted by the same "Deborah Duncan", about entertaining the idea of letting my group, the Red Hat Mamas of Country Place, attend her show. I reminded her of our meeting 16 years earlier. I knew it was 16 years exactly since last year we had our 15th reunion ... Bobbie, Maureen, Chica and I ... at Maureen's house where we watched an old VCR tape of our appearance on the show and toasted with margaritas every time we saw ourselves on TV.

I'll let you know if Deborah remembers me and I get my leftover eleven minutes of fame. Whatever happens happens. That's show biz! Break a leg!

****

The wait is over. In the time it's taken me to get this book finished, I completed my last eleven minutes of fame.

Deborah did let the Red Hatters on her show, then sat down beside me and commented on my painted silk poncho of "Women Who Lunch Wearing Red Hats." When I told her I painted it, she hailed her assistant over and asked her to arrange for a film crew to come to our house and produce a video of silk painting. The filming took five hours and also morphed into a visual tour of the art in our home.

The day the video aired on "Great Day Houston," I invited 30 of my friends from my various activities (tennis, bridge, art, writing, book club, and mah jongg) to sit in the audience modeling my silk ponchos and scarves. What a day!

Thanks to my coffin, Andy, Deborah and my "amigas," I really soaked my 15 minutes to the max!

****

DIGGING THROUGH THE PAST!

My husband and I have traveled the world, especially parts of Mexico, searching for Pre-Columbian sites, artifacts and shards. We've gone on several digs (Texas, Mexico and Spain) searching for signs of early man and his leavings but always had to relinquish our finds to the powers that be to be placed in museums, showrooms or exhibits.

Little did I know that down a Friendswood, Texas street in an unremarkable neighborhood I would wade through trash and find what I had been looking for all along.

It was a garage saleing day like any other, and we (the fearsome four, Bobbie, Maureen, Chica and I) were on our way home with a car load of things we hadn't even known we wanted but soon discovered we couldn't live without. Everyone was tired, anxious to quit and return home to get AC'ed - it was Texas hot - but since I was driving, I had the winning vote and turned into a neighborhood we had already visited earlier that day, but after we left, someone had put up a new garage sale sign.

We had no trouble finding the sale, but there were no cars. It soon became apparent why there were no customers. This was not a sale like any we had seen. The lady of the house had put her tables of trash down the driveway, and they were laden with used Tupperware, various sizes of metal lids for long-ago thrown-out pans, vases formerly holding flowers that had died but she just couldn't part with the cheap glass vases, presents she had received and wanted to get rid of without anybody knowing, and a few old records. This was a drive-by garage sale. Everyone moaned when we saw the tables, but I, believing in providence, said there must have been a reason we turned in here. Everyone moaned again.

We sped-eyed the tables and were turning to leave when the woman said, "Oh, yeah. My husband is selling some things in the garage but I doubt if you'd be interested."

I squinted back into the garage and, oh, what my eyes did behold! A small man stood in front of a table of pure "King-Tut-like" treasures (if he had been an ancient non-royal Aztec) waiting there for me and now I knew what Hiram Bingham must have felt like when he re-found Macchu Picchu. After the preliminary niceties were exchanged, I learned the man standing in my way of these wonderful artifacts had been the owner of a store of PreColumbian antiquities, had recently sold his business and was trying to get rid of the last of his stock.

All of his pieces had been researched and identified and marked with soaring prices. But I reminded him this was a garage sale, and also hinted at the fact that I was the only one I knew of who would be interested in his wares, the others in our group already drifting back to the car.

I'll save you, my reader, the details of the embarrassing bargaining I participated in, but suffice it to say, I was over-the-top happy when I gleefully skipped back down the long driveway, trying not to trip and drop my Aztec blood cup, polished Otomi bowl, several small pieces, and many shards (enough for a fantastic mosaic), all for only a measly $15.

The bowl and the blood cup now reside in our living room display case, along with geodes from Chile, shards from Mexico, 65-to-125-million-year-old dinosaur bones from Utah, and even some dentures I found on the beach of the Black Sea in Romania. When people visit, I love relating the history of the cup and watching my friends cringe at the story of the Aztec rituals. The Aztecs often used obsidian knives or maguey thorns for auto-sacrifice, the letting of one's own blood from themselves or other human beings to be offered to the gods or from animals to be slaughtered. Sometimes with a captured enemy who they admired, they would prick the penis (for fertility) or elsewhere (head for intelligence; heart for valor; arms for strength) and drink their adversary's blood from a cup such as the one I bought. Wow! If only my cup could talk, think of the tales it could tell. Now, if only Hannibal Lecter would stop by for a glass of nice chianti, I'd be ready.

Garage saleing is like a "dig" or a "box of chocolates." You never know what "delicious" prize you're going to find!

****

AND THE LIST GOES ON!

Previously I bragged about my three most-favorite garage sale finds, but here's some other precious possessions that I couldn't have found at Walmart or Macy's:

1. Up in South Bend, Indiana, at a yard sale I found an antique pair of "used" **snowshoes.** When people would wander through our house and ask questions about our decorations, we'd say, "That's from Easter Island. That's from Tanzania. That's from the Amazon." And then they'd point to the snowshoes and we'd say, "That's from a garage sale." Their looks were priceless.

2. Another never-to-get-rid-of treasure: A battery-driven, bug-eyed stuffed **monkey** that straps onto your leg and then, when turned on (literally), he humps your leg while making appropriate turned-on monkey noises. I was garage saleing in San Antonio with my Mormon sister-in-law, Rita Cortez, when we discovered this monkey for only $2, and I didn't want her to think badly of me, so I let him go and left that garage sale empty-handed. But when Art and I got on the road to home a few hours later, I could stand it no longer, the chimp's absence was eating away at my psyche. I called Rita from the road and

she ran over and captured my prize (what a great sister-in-law to have), though I was surprised he was still there, still unadopted. I should have known it was one of those "gotta have its" the minute I saw him and have never regretted my purchase (when I typed this line, I turned my head from the computer and smiled at "Slappy" sitting quietly in his chair in my office; I swear he smiled back).

3. Large **carved gnu horn** from Africa for $5. This may has caused a rift in a couple's marriage, since I heard them arguing when I was leaving with my prize; the man was yelling that he could have sold it on eBay for $100 ... easy! I tucked it inside my coat as I hurried to the car.

4. 30 **Special Olympics gold medals** from a bright young lad who was so proud that I had bought them all from him, with his mother beaming in the background as he told me excitedly how he won each one. A tennis tournament of friends over 60 benefited from this find.

5. 50 colorful **bikinis** (each .50 from separate sales) for decorations at a wedding shower I threw for the bride-to-be (Jennifer Bevan Cobb) who was soon to be married on the beach in Florida. The bikinis were subsequently recycled at a family reunion in Padre Island where the theme was Hawaii and since it is a very large family, we couldn't get into them but pinned them on our clothes to riotous receptions.

6. Large **tortoise shell** (sans tortoise) that I have always intended to paint. But so far he only sits on the ledge of the bathtub in the spare

bathroom collecting dust until we have company and he's soaked.

7. Five **Lladros** (artistic porcelain figurines from Spain that every tourist must purchase to prove they've been to Spain - I already had two so I knew what they cost) each bought at separate sales and each for under $4. Go figure. I just took them and ran.

8. Circular toothed jawbone from the mouth of a **shark**. Albeit a baby (these might be baby-baby shark teeth), he still holds three rolled-up hand towels in his mouth (sadly full of pulled threads), and I do not need a "bigger boat."

9. **Baskets and themed "things"** (For example: One basket with things for teachers, another with over-the-hill stuff, another with cats, one with cards, one with cooking utensils, one with Rated R paraphernalia, ad nauseam). Known locally as the "bag lady," I filled over over 200 cellophane-wrapped baskets with bows (ribbons and cellophane also bought at garage sales) and sold the lot of them ... or a lot of them ... mostly due to the kindness of strangers.

10. Large taxidermied **alligator head** that I used to hold a bar of soap in its jaws in my "primitive" guest bathroom that was also outfitted with **reindeer antlers** (from the Arctic Circle) towel holders.

11. Small taxidermied **smiling alligator**. Years later I invited my friend, Gloria Hander Lyon, who was direly ill and didn't have much longer to live, to come to my mother of all garage sales when we downsized. And she said, "Only if there's a

margarita in it for me," and I told her I was, indeed, serving margaritas. And then she added, "And only if I can find an alligator," and I promised her one. And I elatedly delivered.

12. Various and sundry **voodoo dolls** (none of them worked, apparently you need to add batteries or utter special words).

13. Antique large squash blossom **turquoise necklace** from Mexico for only .50 cents.

14. **Cowhide No. 2.** Years ago I spent $20 on a cowhide knowing that was a great price, so when I saw Cowhide No. 2 for only $10, I simply had to get it but regretted my actions the minute I packed it into the trunk ... no room in the inn. At the next garage sale ten minutes later, I opened my trunk and a fellow garage-saler guy spotted it and offered me $35. I jumped at the chance. He was thrilled and felt he took me, and I felt the same way except in the opposite direction. Win-Win ... except for the cow!

15. Large molded **leather bust** of a woman's head and her bust. This was dusted off the wall of the salers' garage, after telling us its history, regaling us with how much they had enjoyed looking at it, receiving compliments on it and finally telling us the story of the famous artist who conceived it. I knew I couldn't afford it but I went ahead and asked "How much" anyway, just to be nice and friendly. Though stunned when he said, "$2," I didn't, as I did once before, offer him more and ruin the whole process for both of us.

16. Five antique **Mexican Trees of Life** to add to my collection. After that wonderful purchase, I

asked at every garage sale for over five years if they had one, but to no avail. In the words of my fellow garage saler, Bobbie, when I asked for her recollection of special "finds": <u>"Mostly I remember you driving me crazy asking at every sale if they had a tree of life. I would say, 'These people won't have anything like that,' and they never did and after a few years, you finally quit asking. Then a month after you quit cold turkey, you did find a tree of life at a yard sale and started your 'do you have any trees of life' mantra all over again for many more years with no luck until you finally ran out of steam."</u>

17. A plastic male statue with all the acupuncture points written on him which had been previously used to teach the art of acupuncture, along with a book of instructions. I subsequently bought 300 colored-ball straight pins and made an art piece out of him, highlighting all his better points and attaching a small plastic olive leaf covering some that weren't.

****

AND FINALLY ...

FRIENDS' TALES OF "WOE"
AND
"WHOA" MOMENTS!

****

THE ORIGINAL HAPPY MEAL!

Susie West's mother died last year. Susie and her sister wanted to prepare their father his favorite meal for his 75th birthday. They confab'ed about what to prepare, and then simultaneously remembered that for all holidays and his birthday, their mother made him a dish she had invented with hamburger, okra and whole tomatoes over rice with her secret sauce.

So, it was decided that for his first birthday in 50 years without his wife, they would surprise him with that concoction. They worked hard replicating his special meal and giggled about how happy he would be when they served it to him on their parents' old Melmac dishes.

When they laid the feast out before him, he threw down his napkin and said, "Damn-it. I hate this dish and the plate it came in on. I've eaten that horrible stuff on that same horrible plate for 50 years ... only for your mother ... and I'm never, never going to eat it again. She made it on our honeymoon and I told her it was the most delicious thing I ever tasted and I've had to eat it ever since. But I'm calling a stop to that nonsense right now!!!! And, girls, throw away those nasty plates!"

The sisters exploded in laughter and immediately got out the paper plates and Susie called for carry-out pizza from his favorite restaurant (they knew it was his favorite since that's where he would take them when their mother left him in charge and he always made them promise they wouldn't give it away because he had instructions from her to take them to Luby's for a "sensible dinner").

They loved him telling them the story of his honeymoon, a modern day O'Henry's "Gift of the Magi" tale about the hair and the watch fob, and they loved him even more for making their mother happy for so long. Good-bye, Okra Winfrey!

****

COMPUTER MISCHIEF!

Dawn Storey's story (yes, that's really my fellow writer's name): Delaina, her daughter, came home briefly one Friday for lunch. While Dawn was in the kitchen preparing their meal, Delaina asked if she could use Dawn's phone to let her college roommate know where she was. Before hanging up, she noticed that Dylan, her brother, had texted their mother about something or other and a devilish plan was born.

She wrote to Dylan: "I'm sorry to have to tell you this over the phone, but it will make it easier for me. You are adopted. If you have any questions, just let me know or else you can keep it to yourself and we'll never mention it again. Sorry."

Dawn thought it funny that all during their lunch together, Delaina looked like a cat who ate the canary, she could hardly control her giggles, but they had a good talk and as she was getting ready to leave, she told Dawn to be sure to check her texts that evening as she would probably be hearing again from Dylan.

Dawn knew something was amiss and rushed to her phone only to find a message marked "Urgent" from her son. He seemed to figure out things as he wrote, and it started with: "Why didn't you ever tell me"... and ended with: Did Delaina come to visit you today?"

Dawn wrote back, "Yes," with a smiley face!

****

BLIND LEADING THE COLOR BLIND!

I was having trouble deciding on a color to paint our living room, so I got five samples of paints - red, brown, green, orange and yellow - and painted six broad rectangles (about 12X12 inches each) up a wall. Art and I were even more confused then by that system I devised and still at odds on which to pick.

Mary Helen Lowry came to visit the next day, and I decided, starting with her, to take a survey and go with the consensus. I showed her the wall and she said, "Stripes! Who would have thought it! I love it!"

We chose the orange without consulting further survey participants.

****

EDITH AND MABEL!

This story was told to me by two friends, giggling throughout their rendition, who have threatened me within an inch of my life if I reveal their names; ergo, here's the story of "Edith and Mabel."

Two elderly matrons opted to enjoy a light lunch at the neighborhood pink-themed tearoom. After being led to their seats at a dainty wrought iron ice cream table by a young lady in an antebellum dress topped by a large flower-festooned hat, they sat down, closed their eyes and inhaled the aroma of fresh baked bread and smiled. Memories.

Edith and Mabel were sisters but better than that, they were friends. Graciously accepting their menus, Mabel looked around the corner of hers and spotted another table over Edith's shoulder where sat two very old ladies. "Look at that, Edith. Wait! No, don't look now. I don't know when they sat down since I didn't see them when we came in. But ... no, don't look ... the oldest one is facing me and fondling her pearls like she's afraid the waitress is going to steal them! And whoever told her she looked good in that dress ought to be crucified. It sort of looks like mine but doesn't fit her as well. What is our world coming to? She just keeps talking and talking and won't let the other lady speak. Not that that one would ever have anything interesting to say since she's dressed like she's ready for a wake ... hers! Her hair is a total disgrace with its wildness. She probably hasn't heard of a hairdresser for all that blue fuzz. And by the looks of it, her too-tight wrinkled dress is on its last outing. And didn't her mother ever tell her to sit up straight, she slouches like you do. Oh, sorry, I didn't mean that but ... no, don't look. I mean it!"

After Mabel's tirade, she glared hard at the other table, then calmed down a bit and lowered her head. Looking down at her gloved hands, with practiced grace, she slowly removed her left and then her right glove. She smoothed her napkin down on her lap and looked up again. "Oh, my Gawd, Edith. Our waitress is going to their table to get their order before us. I can't believe that! Should we leave or talk to the manager? We were here before them and they're going to get served before us??? Okay. You can look now, but just stare all three of them down until they get the hint, okay?"

Edith sighed and said, "Mabel, Honey, put on your glasses. That's a mirror! The waitress is waiting. Now let's order!"

****

PLAYING CAT & MOUSE!

While driving in to Houston for tennis one day with my friend, Bobbie, I noticed that her hands were shaking and just had to ask why, since I knew there was a story there. She said it was nothing, she was just a little shaken, but I smelled a rat. I knew she had nerves of steel. But as she told her story, I realized that although her nerves are hard, her heart is soft.

For quite some time now, she had been caring for a cat that wandered around outside her house every day and would not leave. Bobbie said she tried hard, but she couldn't get rid of it. I asked, "Do you feed it?" She said, "Yeah, but only because I don't want it to starve." I hated to tell her that in the first few seconds of her story, I knew the answer to her question of why it wouldn't leave. She had been talking about the cat that she didn't like ever since it arrived a year ago, bragging about its feats of brilliance and its genius in following commands. She just had to face it: She had a cat! And she liked the cat!

Then she started her story. Her husband, Ed, was really angry that this cat was no mouser and wasn't earning its keep, especially since it was eating them out of house and home (a tad exaggerated but she said he was mad when they saw a mouse for the third time in the cat's garage ... yes, it had the run of the whole garage). If that wasn't bad enough, it was where they saw him ... playing with their cat on the cat's pillow. The feline batted him around, pawed and played with him, and he'd jump and come back for more. Bobbie thought it odd that the cat would have a pet of her own, but then it hit her. It was no pet; it was a ... eek! ... mouse!

Bobbie had been on the lookout for the mouse for a week with no luck. Then she figured if she cleaned out the garage, it would be harder for him to stay there, so she got the vacuum out and headed to the garage. Mid-sweep, she spotted the critter with the cat nowhere to be found. She headed straight for him vacuum in hand, took off the cleaner head and pointed the tube at the culprit. She got down closer. **SLURRRPPP!** The sound was deafening as the mouse was sucked into the vacuum cleaner's bowels. Actually they weren't bowels, but a clear plastic container on the side of the vacuum, sort of like its colostomy bag. It jumped and skittered in there among the dust balls, squeaking loudly until she could take no more and headed for her kitchen to settle down and call her grandson to come take care of it.

Daniel Jones, the grandson/knight/savior of the story, arrived about five hours later. They went out to the garage and found the vacuum right where Bobbie left it, but the mouse was nowhere to be seen. There was no way for him to escape and yet he was gone. Not Mickey but Magic Mickey! Daniel took off the hose and slammed it back shut. The mouse was in the shaft trying to get out. Now, Bobbie couldn't kill the little fellow, but screamed at Daniel to do the dirty deed. But being raised by Bobbie, he must have learned a trait or two and said he just couldn't kill it either. They looked at the cat. The cat couldn't either. Finally Daniel decided to take Magic Mick to a nearby park. So, he finagled it out of the tube and Ubered it on its merry way to an exciting new life.

While Daniel was rodent-relocating, Bobbie tried to clean up the space and noticed her homeless cat in the corner happily playing one-sided badminton with another ... what? ... mouse!

And the drama continues. Will Mick find its way back home? Will Bobbie ever admit she likes a cat who likes mice? Will Ed ever get fed before the cat? Will Daniel refuse to answer his phone any more? Will the mouse family find a new garage or move to the big house in a coup? To be continued.

****

WAY TO GO, GIRLS!

My mah jongg friend, Edwina Peyton, one day soon after her husband's funeral, read to us his written instructions for his "going-away" party ("Don't let Herb drink too much. Sit Helen far away from Evelyn. Don't serve anything with onion in it" - he hated the smell. "Get really cute waitresses and tip them big") and included a hundred dollar bill for a keg of beer for the reception. Apparently he wrote his request many years earlier when a hundred dollars really bought you something. We all agreed how creative and wonderful it was of him to make all the arrangements before his demise to help Edwina.

Then she told us about her friends who did something along the same lines. They had a "funeral planning" party with lots of wine and expressed how they wanted their "after-life" celebrations handled, what they wanted said and what they'd like to be handed out at their respective funerals.

I thought this such a grand idea, I adopted it as my own and had a Day of the Dead party for my friends. I should have guessed the requests of some. Betsy Miller, the artist, wants crayons and paper distributed to the attendees. Avril Forster, the pilot, wants her ashes scattered from here to Canada, her first home. My cousin, Butch Richardson, wanted his widow to serve popcorn. Sami Lee wants everyone to get a new tennis ball. And I want margaritas served at my "celebration of it all" party with my friends modeling my silk ponchos.

I've even already written my obituary but I don't want to jinx things and print it here in case the powers that be take things literally, but the first sentence of it is the last sentence of this book.

****

CULTURE SHOCK!

For a year, I organized and ran a "culture club." We weren't picky about what constituted "culture" and enjoyed bowling just as much as a lectured tour of Houston's architecture, rhapsodized over a concert and cheered at the racetracks. It was a good, diverse group of women just wanting to have fun and learn something at the same time.

When the Impressionists came to town, I figured it was a perfect opportunity to get in our obligatory visit to the Museum of Fine Arts, Houston (MFAH). One friend, Sharon Guss, was a fabulous tennis player, common-sensical beauty, but a country girl throughout, and she had never been to an art museum. In fact, she thought I was cursing when I told her we were going to the MFAH.

Since I knew a few trivia tidbits about art, I decided to take Sharon under my wig and share with her the special qualities of some of the artists that I had learned from my very own mentor, Betsy Miller, and guide her through the museum.

It was a fabulous collection, everyone was there ... Toulouse-Lautrec, Degas, Manet, Monet, Pissarro, Renoir ... and at the outset, I told Sharon the names of the artists she had to look forward to.

"Oh," she said, "I thought with those names, you were talking about a foreign car collection." (I told you she was smart). She was kidding, of course ... or was she? And on we went through the decorated halls.

I explained about Degas' love of ballerinas, Toulouse-Lautrec's obsession with the cabaret scene (he painted bright posters of advertising), Monet's passion with the water lily (he coined the name "Impressionism"), Renoir using his wife as a model in my favorite, "Luncheon of the Boating Party" and how during his last 20 years of life he was wheelchair-bound and later painted by having a brush strapped to his paralyzed fingers. Such dedication. And on and on I went.

At the end of our three hours of adoration and amazement, having been sufficiently sated with culture, we all gathered at the Cafe Express to discuss our enthusiasm. We sat down at a round table and had an actual discussion ... all were impressed with impressionism, it seems. Ineke asked Sharon how she had enjoyed the paintings.

"They were absolutely, absolutely wonderful," Sharon responded. And I smugly smiled, so proud was I of my student.

But then she continued, "Those were the most magnificent **frames** I have ever seen in my life!!!"

****

****

NOW THAT'S ENOUGH "LITTLE HELP"

FROM MY FRIENDS. THE

FOLLOWING

PAGES ARE THE END, LITERALLY!!!!!

****

A FRUITFUL LIFE!

Our friend, Bob Faust, had pancreatic cancer. He had been taking chemo for six months and was the sole surviving participant in an experimental test program at the local cancer center in Houston, Texas. But he knew ... and we knew ... his time amongst us was limited.

Nevertheless, when Art and I asked him if he wanted to take a driving trip to Mexico, he emphatically said, "Yes." Of course, his wife, Debbie, wanted to do whatever he wanted to do, so she was all for it. Bob's doctors felt the same way, and they removed his chemo port, taped it over and wished him a good trip.

So, after Christmas of 2000, with the ominous cloud of Bob's imminent death looming over us and the optimistic promise of a new year awaiting us, we headed off on a Mexican adventure.

Death rode with us and was the elephant in the car. We all were outwardly, awkwardly jolly and wanted to make this time special, but it was Bob who managed to do that for us. When we crossed the Tropic of Cancer, I begged for a photo stop, Art braked, Debbie laughed, and Bob groaned out the words, "Cancer, oh, no." The car was silent and then we all began roaring at his joke.

The four of us were bird-watchers (some more than others) but in the Mexican high plains, birds are sometimes few and far between. But Art had heard tell of a cemetery near the highway where people had spotted some special birds. As we pulled into the brilliantly-flowered cemetery oasis, the screeching and cawing from the trees was deafening, loud enough to wake the dead. And when we got out of the car to get a better look, Bob raised his fist up to the buzzards circling in the brilliant blue sky. He took a Scarlet O'Hara stance, then screamed at them, "Go away! You can't have me yet!" Again, he brought down the house and we giggled at his black humor.

Our days were filled with laughter and fun, with Bob showing us the way it was. On another foray into bird-watching, while returning from a trip to Tamazunchale, Art spotted some darting color in an orange orchard and veered onto a private dirt road off the main highway. The bird-watching was incredible and we stayed for a half-hour enjoying the winged world through our binoculars. It wasn't long, though, before we realized "we" were also being watched. A black truck slowly approached us as we eased back to our Suburban for the safety of numbers and the inside of our vehicle.

Sure enough, it was the landowner with two of his workers wanting to know our purpose for trespassing. Art pled our innocence to the stern-faced landowner/judge, while the non-Spanish-speakers among us awaited our fate in silent anxiety. Finally, after a second or two of uncertainty, a smile lit the man's face and he graciously welcomed us to Mexico and to his land. Spreading his arms wide open, he announced, "Mi huerto es su huerto" ("My orchard is your orchard"). He invited us to continue with our avian pursuits and then instructed his men to bring us two buckets of "naranjas" - the most delicious oranges this side of Valencia. We overdosed on these juicy morsels, especially Bob, who savored every bite.

We celebrated New Year's Eve at a party in Valles with the locals who soon became our friends, since Bob never met a stranger in his life. We stayed at the gala until the eating of the grapes - downing one grape for each chime during the countdown to midnight. Afterwards, the fiesta continued in our room. Bob had bought and brought with him four bottles of expensive champagne that begged to be drunk -- as did we! We did our best, but only managed to finish two bottles before we took to our beds.

We left the next day for home. It was at the border that we realized that we had more than 20 of the oranges left that we could not take back across the border due to Customs' insistence on inspected fruit. Plus, though we had given it a good high school try, we were unable to finish the last two bottles of champagne the night before. The bottles had no tax stamp, so we weren't allowed to return with them either. Art pulled off the highway, conceding our place in the long line through Customs, and we held an impromptu memorial for our trip, reliving the experiences and laughter that had prevailed. Bob ceremoniously brought out the fruit and bottles of bubbly. As we sat huddled in the car with the heater running, we toasted Bob at every gulp, down to the last drop, until we could finally carry the oranges and champagne across the border legally, albeit internally.

As the Suburban merged back into the line of traffic, glass in hand, Bob gleefully said, "When life hands you oranges, make mimosas!" And he had shown us how.

****

PASSING AWAY OR PASSING THROUGH??

I cringed when Butch Richardson, my cousin in Wichita, Kansas, passed the phone to Brenda, his wife, for me to talk to her, after just informing me she was now on hospice and did not have much longer to live. What would I say? I needn't have worried. Brenda put me at ease right away. She had been handling her plight for five long years, and had given it a good head-to-head fight but the cancer had taken the lead several weeks earlier, and that was all it needed; it took off running and didn't look back.

Hospice was now administering Brenda strong doses of morphine, and though she was somewhat hard to understand, she still retained her cheery and philosophical attitude. "Hi, Marilyn. Glad you called. How are you?"

"All right," I answered. "But what about you?" I asked.

"Well, we all have to die some time," she said matter-of-factly. I had heard this phrase many times before, but never from the source, and never when it meant as much to the one who uttered that old adage. "I just happen to know when it's going to happen. But I won't feel any pain. I will just go to sleep, which is how everyone wants to go." Wow! No wonder Butch had said she was handling this phase of her disease like a true champion.

"Have you talked to Kathleen?" I asked. Kathleen was another cousin living in Wichita who was also on hospice. At 86 years of age, Kathleen had opted to be discharged from the hospital so she could go home and would seek no future treatment. And with hospice care, she was, as she said, living on borrowed time.

"Yeah. We talked of heaven," Brenda said, "She told me that when I get there, to look for her. She'll be following me there, but I may not recognize her. She said she'll be the one with curly hair!" How marvelous that they both could have such a sense of humor at this dire time in their lives. Kathleen had always coveted curly hair, she of the straight-as-an-arrow hair and bangs. She felt that when you die, your deepest wishes come true. I loved the idea. Count me in for a voice like Barbra Streisand, hair like Farrah Fawcett and a defined chin, not quite like Jay Leno's, but one with absolutely no trace of a turkey wattle.

A week after I last talked to Brenda, we were on our way to Wichita when I received a call from Butch saying she had passed that afternoon. He told me that she had been unable to respond for two days. The night before he had been watching the TV sitcom "How I Met Your Mother," in bed with Brenda. The characters in the show were celebrating a birthday and the group sang "Happy Birthday." When the program was over, Butch turned off the TV and Brenda said her last words, "Happy Birthday."

Brenda and Kathleen had it all figured out. They would have a rebirth - so it really was her birthday - and enter into another plane, universe, dimension, time, strata, whatever you want to call it. And it was not a bad place. They would not be passing away; they were just passing through!

****

BUTCH!

Butch, my cousin, died unexpectedly in 2013 - he was always the same age as me and now he's stopped counting. His wife died two years before he did, but he had met another woman and was embarking on a wonderful new life. Below is the first article I wrote right after I heard of his demise and sent it to my friends to let them know I would be gone for a while, traveling to Wichita, Kansas, for the funeral, plus I wanted to get his story down on paper. Following that is the obituary he, himself, personally wrote for the paper (I was impressed and mad that I didn't think of that before him, but you can bet your booty I wrote mine on the long drive back from Wichita). The third is what the Wichita paper wrote the day after his obit appeared, since they had gotten so many phone calls, pro and con, about his obituary. He would have loved it. His body went to Kansas City where they harvested his organs and his skin had already been donated to someone by the next day. A life well lived.

1.   The story:

I never had a brother but my cousin, John (we called him Butch) Richardson, sufficed. We were separated in age by only four months and we conveniently had his younger brother to pick on so we were quite close. Anyway, he married a wonderful woman, Brenda, and they were happily married until 2006 when they discovered she had ovarian cancer. Since she was a nurse, she fought it mightily. Butch was always happy-go-lucky and I was really surprised when he stepped up to the plate and was a devoted, caring and overly attentive nurse to her. I was proud of him. She lost her battle after many long years, living with a colostomy bag for her last year. He was devastated. But he went back to his hobbies: He was a docent at a Frank Lloyd Wright house, ran the trolley city tour for Wichita, worked at the old library cleaning and setting the town clock, and kept himself busy and off the streets.

Three months after he had buried Brenda, John (when he was in an authority position, "Butch" just didn't sound right) was speaking to a nature conservatory of scouts when he keeled over with a massive heart attack and couldn't be revived. The doctors put him on ice for three days to let the swelling go down and then gradually thawed him out to find out if he was still in there. He was.

After a week of recovery, the doctors decided to do open heart surgery with a quadruple bypass. He fought his way back to normality with all the therapy, etc. After he'd recuperated for two months, Art and I traveled to Wichita, to throw him a "Happy to be Alive" fiesta (my suitcase was loaded with serapes, a slow cooker, tortillas, portadas, tamales, etc.). I took flowers for the women's hair and hot pepper ties for the men since I had sent Butch a tie and a letter each week of his recovery. All his friends attended. Then he set about building his life once again.

In October 2013, I received a short e-mail from him saying: "Hope you had a happy birthday. I have asked an older woman to marry me, so I can be like my role model, ART!" I couldn't believe it. He had always called me a cougar for marrying Art six years younger than me, and now, at 71 years of age, he was going to marry an "OLDER WOMAN"??? Gyla Roberson was born in 1938, three years older than him; she lost her husband a week before Brenda died; she was a neighbor and brought Butch over a dish (never underestimate the power of casseroles).

I wrote to tell him how thrilled I was with his news. After that, he wrote me every week, such joyous and giddy and silly letters saying things like: "I asked Gyla to be my wife and have given her a letter jacket so the world knows we are going steady." "She has agreed that we will have no children of our own, which I think is a good decision." "We share an enjoyment of many activities and both dislike dusting." "I will become a Presbyterian and have started with presbyopia in my eyes." "The best part is: She told me she was rich and I wouldn't have to go find a job." "I am very happy right now emotionally and my cardiologist and GP can find little wrong except the mental disorder." "She said she is rich but does not share well with others and I suspect she also runs with scissors." "I take inspiration from your Auntie Mame view of the world. Let's have a little Christmas." "Disagreement has reared its ugly head. Gyla says now she doesn't want to go to Cherokee for our honeymoon. She is interested in a tour of the Star Lumber warehouse. I'd rather go to Peabody and tour the Coop Elevator and watch the awnings rust on the Safeway Grocery. She will probably get her way. Such is married life."

In other words, he was over-the-top happy. They set the merging date for December 3, 2013. He liked the numbers aligned: 12-3-2013. They put their wedding announcement in the paper with a photo that looked like they were celebrating their 50th Anniversary.

On January 2nd Gyla left him to run errands, returning two hours later to find him on the bathroom floor; paramedics could not revive him. We are going to Wichita now to a funeral instead of a wedding. It was so very sad. But for a time, they were unbelievably happy and like kids starting a new life.

Like I said, the moral of the story is: Never take a day for granted, seize happiness. Gyla wore her wedding dress to the funeral and looked strikingly lovely as she served the popcorn my cousin had requested to be served. Since Butch cast me in the role of Auntie Mame, I'll share my favorite quote from that play uttered by Agnes Gooch: "Life is a banquet and most poor suckers are starving to death."

2. The obituary that appeared in the newspaper ... he wrote it himself after he had his first heart attack:

John Dennis Richardson Notice

Richardson, John Dennis, 71, was born at a very early age in Wichita, KS to Eli V. and Faye E. Jackson Richardson at 5:58 am, on August 19, 1941. He grew progressively older until he stopped on September 14, 2011, at the age of 70. He resumed life one week later after quadruple by-pass surgery. Graduating from WHS East in 1959, he received both Bachelor and Master degrees from Wichita State University. Taking a cut in pay, he left Farha Brothers Grocery to become a middle-level social studies teacher for the Wichita Public Schools, retiring in 2001. A facilitator for the teaching of geography at the University of Colorado in Boulder, he became interested in environmental studies and became a facilitator for Project Learning Tree, Wild and Aquatic. In retirement, he pursued his interest in local history becoming a docent for the Wichita-Sedgwick County Historical Museum, the Allen-Lambe House Museum and the Historic Trolley Tours. A Fellow of the National Association of Watch and Clock Collectors, he was one of five trained to maintain the tower clock from 1985 until 2010. He also served as a volunteer and Board member at the Great Plains Nature Center. John was preceded in death by his parents, Eli V. and Faye Edna Richardson; brother, Wallace Darrel; his buddy, Brenda, to whom he was happily married for six of 38 years. Survivors include brother, Richard (Sandi) Richardson, and fianceé, Gyla. John was a new member of

Trinity Presbyterian Church, 2258 Marigold, where Memorial Services will be at 3 pm Sunday, Jan. 6, 2013. There will be no public viewing. Memorials to: GPNC, WSCHM, NAWCC, and the Kansas Humane Society in lieu of flowers. Share online condolences at www.CozineMemorial.com . Services by Broadway Mortuary.

3. The newspaper received so many complaints and inquiries about the obituary that they had to write an explanation the next day (I wish it had been a retraction, though):

John Richardson had the last laugh

His obituary in The Eagle is rife with humor.

John Dennis Richardson, 71, was "born at a very early age," the remembrance says. "He grew progressively older until he stopped on Sept. 14, 2011, at the age of 70. He resumed life one week later after quadruple bypass surgery."

Mr. Richardson was "happily married for six of 38 years," his obituary goes on. Friends say Mr. Richardson, who died this week, had a great sense of humor.

"I highly suspect he wrote that himself," Eric Cale, executive director of the Wichita-Sedgwick Historical

Museum, where Mr. Richardson volunteered, said of the obituary. Indeed, he did, a family member said.

Mr. Richardson, born in Wichita, was a longtime volunteer, offering his time not only to the historical museum but also the Allen-Lambe House Museum and the Great Plains Nature Center. He led historic trolley tours and was one of only five people trained to maintain the clock in the bell tower at the historical museum. Mr. Richardson was a fellow of the National Association of Watch and Clock Collectors. "He was probably the most stalwart of the clock volunteers, in my memory, anyway," Cale said. Cale remembered a time when a hand on the clock came loose, and Mr. Richardson went to great pains to get it fixed.

"Imagine Harold Lloyd," Cale said, alluding to the actor shown hanging from a clock in the silent movie "Safety Last!" It wasn't quite that dramatic, but Cale said he could imagine Richardson in that type of scene.

"His main work here was either with the clock or with our education department in providing tours," Cale said.

Mr. Richardson helped train other people to care for the clock in the bell tower, Cale said. "He had a succession plan," Cale said.

Mr. Richardson earned bachelor's and master's degrees from Wichita State University. His obituary says he took a cut in pay when he left Farha Brothers Grocery to become a social studies teacher. He retired in 2001.

Although the obituary jokes about his marriage, Mr. Richardson stood by his wife, Brenda, as she fought cancer, Cale said. She preceded him in death. "He ushered her through all types of treatment over the years," Cale said.

Mr. Richardson suffered a heart attack while volunteering at the nature center. The bit in his obit about how he "resumed life" after surgery — that was true, Cale said.

Bob Gress, former director of the nature center, said Mr. Richardson's heart attack occurred during the Kids Care About Nature three-day program. "He was a volunteer instructor, and he had a heart attack at that event," Gress said. "His heart stopped and everything. EMS was able to get him back. I visited him at the hospital later, and they literally had him on ice. He had no recollection of that whole week, period." Gress called Mr. Richardson a "great volunteer," the type who "was always there when you needed him."

Mr. Richardson also served two terms on the board of directors for the Friends of the Great Plains Nature Center, Gress said.

****

****

Thanks to Butch, I've now been inspired and have written my own obituary for long-term, future use, the first line of which is:

"Although her wigs, bionic eyes, pinned

toe, artificial knees, hearing aids and

Pacemaker outlived her, she still had

a good run!"

****